& COLLECTIBLES

IDENTIFICATION AND VALUE GUIDE

DAVID LONGEST

COLLECTOR BOOKS

A Division of Schroeder Publishing Co., Inc.

The current values in this book should be used only as a guide. They are not intended to set prices, which vary from one section of the country to another. Auction prices as well as dealer prices vary greatly and are affected by condition as well as demand. Neither the author nor the publisher assumes responsibility for any losses that might be incurred as a result of consulting this guide.

Searching for a Publisher?

We are always looking for knowledgeable people considered to be experts within their fields. If you feel that there is a real need for a book on your collectible subject and have a large comprehensive collection, contact Collector Books.

On the cover:

Cartoon Toys from the 1930s, 1940s, 1950s, and 1960s. All toys pictured on cover are priced and described in this book.

Cover design: Beth Summers
Book design: Kent Henry

Collector Books
P.O. Box 3009
Paducah, KY 42002-3009

CONTENTS

ACKNOWLEDGMENTS

First of all, this author would like to thank Lisa Stroup at Collector Books for being the world's most patient editor. Her silence as I missed each extended deadline was golden. Lisa, you're great! And I know the patience you've learned from your procrastinating authors will make you an even greater mom. Congratulations on your new little one. And to Billy Schroeder, my publisher, I say "thanks again...and again." Collector Books' faith in me, which has now lasted for 16 years (has it really been that long?) and sustained me through this sixth book, is always appreciated. If every prospective author out there knew how great you guys are to work for, you'd have to build a warehouse just for the new manuscripts.

Also, I would like to thank the many collectors who allowed me to be a part of the family for at least one day as we did the photo shoot. To Ron Flick and family, thanks for allowing me to spend a fun but hectic winter Sunday running up and down the stairs of your beautiful Indiana Victorian home. Your children are precious and they were quite entertaining while I photographed your (or their?) toys. My thanks to you, your wife, and kids. To Mike Sullivan and Gina Lightle of As Time Goes By Antiques in Louisville, Kentucky, thanks for putting up with me crowding into your wonderful shop. Thanks for being the good people and great friends that you are, and also thanks for the great Disneyana you've sold me over the years...even on the day I shot the toys in your store!

To Doug Moore of Cicero, Indiana, thanks for letting me move in on that winter Saturday. I'd always wanted to see your collection, so the visit allowed me to both see and "shoot" it all in one day. You're one of the world's greatest guys...and collectors, Doug. May your planned retirement next year be all that you want it to be. Just don't find all the antique toys left in the Midwest as you travel. Leave a few for me. Also, to Inez Real of New Albany, Indiana, thanks for letting me mess up your living room on that snowy winter night when we eventually got that record breaking 23". Not much of a night for toys, but the Ninja Turtles stayed warm and dry. What a collection you have! And thanks for being the friend you are and absolutely the world's best bookkeeper!

To Terry Stewart, I owe a lot. It was your family's giant flea markets in Louisville, Kentucky, that got me hooked on toy collecting in the first place. And several times you have allowed me into your home to photograph your wonderful Popeye toys and comic collectibles, I have been increasingly amazed at their quality, rarity, and condition. Keep those bigger and better flea markets from Stewart Promotions coming, and you know I'll be at every one (sneaking in before I'm supposed to be there). Thanks for letting your collection be a part of this book!

And to Glenn Edwards of Evansville, Indiana (or is it Glenn Evans of Edwardsville?), what can I say? You have been a true friend through thick and thin and been a pal at all those shows when I loaded my trunk with Disney and you left empty handed...with no Bugs. May this book help you find some more Bugs pals, and may lots of folks out there start letting the good old Warner Brothers toys hit the market.

Now, to Elmer and Viola Reynolds, how do I say thanks once again? There's never been a book I've done that you haven't been a part of, and your toys have once again been shared with the world. After so many years and so many memories, you are not just friends now, you are family. I thank you for that friendship and for your love. You have made toy collecting, and sharing, one of the great things in life. You're the best!

Finally, to my wife, Ann, and eleven-year-old daughter, Claire, I say thanks for being understanding when I tied up the phone lines with the Internet for days, and missed out on more than a fair share of family outings. Thanks for all that you both do for me every day (like ignoring the mess that three floodlights, four tripods, six colored backgrounds, 500 scattered sheets of paper, 875 randomly assorted photographs, and dozens of toys off their shelves can make in one room). If the Blue Fairy could wave a magic wand and give me the best wife and daughter that I could ever have...you two would always reappear again and again. I love you both and thanks for putting up with one more book.

I dedicate this book to my family and friends...so to Ann, Claire, Juanita and Al, Bea, Jane and Dave, Kristin, Kassie, and Kyle, Dale, Mendy, Brittany and Kelsey, Angela, Andrew and Alex, Glenn and Jean, Bette and Kahler, Lee, Elmer and Viola, and everybody else I forgot since I've had four Diet Cokes already and my brain is a little pickled...

This one's for you.

INTRODUCTION

Ever since the invention of the earliest movie cameras around the turn of the century, film directors have experimented with filming characters that are magically brought to life on the screen by the phenomenon of frame-by-frame animation photography.

At first, film animation was nothing more than a weird photographic novelty, with little thought given to any sort of plot or character development. The first animated images were little more than line-drawn puppets who danced about in jerky motion on screen. But by the time Walt Disney introduced Mickey Mouse in 1928 with the first-ever sound cartoon "Steamboat Willie," animation was already a hot commodity recognized by Hollywood as fun, if not brief, entertainment.

With Betty Boop, Oswald the Rabbit, Felix the Cat and Ignatz the Mouse, early Mickey Mouse, and Popeye cartoons all making their film character debuts in the 1920s and 1930s, Hollywood studios latched onto this new-found entertainment medium as a quick way to boost theatre audiences for their regular live-action studio releases. In essence, the form of the movie cartoon short film was born because studios knew that these animated films were a cheap way to fill time slots between double features, intermissions, and film promotional trailers.

With the advent of early television programming in the late 1940s and early 1950s, local stations and national networks also recognized the importance of cartoons. The 1950s and the 1960s witnessed a virtual onslaught of old animated cartoon re-releases being transferred from the silver screen to the picture tube all in a quick effort to fill the countless hours needed for children's programming. Although locally produced clown shows, story hours, and birthday clubs sprang up all across America in the 1950s, producers quickly discovered that an easy way to fill time slots for the "kiddies" was to slap an old cartoon on the film projector and let it roll! (One often wonders what those early television clowns, puppeteers, and story ladies did while the five-to seven-minute cartoons rolled.) Needless to say, cartoons caught on with the young television audiences, and as the Walt Disney Studios quickly discovered, cartoons were great for both movies and television.

While Walt Disney's artists continually churned out a full-length animated feature every year or two from 1938 on, they also continued rigorous work on short cartoon subjects starring the likes of Mickey Mouse, Donald Duck, Goofy, and Chip and Dale to fill the needs at both movie theaters for their Disney Studios full-length feature film releases and their newborn television shows "Disneyland" and "The Mickey Mouse Club."

Through Disney's incredible success story with cartoon technology and artist development, audiences became more and more demanding for increased animated film production. Who would have thought that Hanna-Barbera Studios could fill an evening network time slot with its newly released "Flintstones" series in the 1960s when those same cartoon characters would have to go head-to-head in the ratings wars against some of the greatest television westerns and sit-coms series ever produced?

But cartoons were here to stay, and the subsequent popularity of Hanna-Barbera's "Flintstones," "Huckleberry Hound and Quick Draw McGraw," and "The Jetsons" series all helped to make family viewing of animated films an American way of life.

Over three generations of Americans have now grown up watching cartoons as a form of both childhood and adult family entertainment. And over this 80 year meteoric rise in the popularity of animated film subjects, the phenomenon of cartoon character merchandising has quickly followed the public's demand for toys designed in the likenesses of the cartoon characters it so genuinely loves. Literally billions of dollars have been spent on cartoon character toys and collectibles this century, and this book is only a seemingly small, almost microscopic look at some of the toys that have found their way into the toy boxes of the children (and adults) across America who so dearly love their favorite cartoon characters.

As a collector, I have had an on-going craziness about Mickey Mouse and Donald Duck for the past 23 years. But as a child, it was Huckleberry Hound and Quick Draw McGraw who threw me for a loop! For some six or seven years of my childhood, it was Quick Draw's sidekick Baba Looey who was my bedtime pal in the form of a plush toy, so cartoons have been very much a part of both my childhood and adult life.

And the toys inspired by all the great cartoons will always be a part of me. Cartoon toys are a fun, colorful, innocent diversion available to all of us who still have that unbroken link between childhood fantasy and adult reality. The toys help us keep that link healthy and continuous.

May life always be so fine. Enjoy your tour through almost 1,000 pictorial examples of cartoon playthings. May you each find something that kindles a spark in your memory of a fond, very young, childhood day!

David Longest, February, 1998

DISNEY CARTOON CHARACTER COLLECTIBLES

The most famous animated cartoon character of all time is undoubtedly Mickey Mouse. When Walt Disney first introduced the bratty little rodent to movie screens back in 1928, Mickey wasn't the first cartoon to appear on screen, as many believe. There had been plenty of earlier animation work going on during the early 1920s. What Disney did with Mickey was introduce an actual "acting" film animation character with a personality all his own, and Walt topped it all off with a cute little falsetto voice for the little rodent who could also sing and whistle. When "Steamboat Willie" was introduced to the public as the first true sound cartoon, Mickey Mouse was an overnight hit! Walt knew he was on to something.

Minnie Mouse was there by Mickey's side from the first early Mickey cartoons, and quickly the cast of characters began to grow. By 1930, Walt was using dozens of animal characters to fill up his "stable" of actors for short cartoons.

By the mid-1930s, a man known still by Disneyana Collectors entered the picture and convinced Walt that Mickey Mouse could bring the new studio extra dollars by the merchandising of Mickey and Minnie Mouse into toys, dolls, books, clothes, and whatever other marketable items could be imagined. That man was Kay Kaymen. Collectors may still find his name associated with distribution of many very early Disney cartoon character toys.

And so, the Disney marketing pipeline was opened full force, and the funds have never stopped flowing. Disney marketing genius quickly matched Disney studio artistry, and the two have remained a match made in animation heaven. The high quality films of the Disney Studios promote the sale of toys in the likeness of Disney characters, and the fine quality licensed toy products help promote the popularity of the studios' characters. Things could not have worked out better.

Collectors of Disneyana today have almost unlimited resources for collecting. Some collectors buy only new and limited edition merchandise. Other collectors of Disney toys focus only on items associated with the theme parks or the annual Disneyana collector conventions. Still others narrow their collecting range to films and characters from only one decade of studio production, such as characters and toys from the 1930s or the 1950s.

Whatever the interest of a particular collector, the field of Disneyana is a wide open one. There are incredible bargains to be found in collecting new merchandise since there is simply so much of it in the marketplace to be purchased. With literally tons of Disney merchandise out there to be bought by the public daily, prices for new items remain very reasonable.

Although vintage Mickey Mouse and Minnie Mouse items from the 1930s have seen their prices skyrocket over the past two decades, even these toys have become more accessible to the new collector in recent years as older collectors who once sought out only the toys from their childhood era (the 1930s) have been selling their collections in the past 10 years as they enter retirement or their estates are sold. This doesn't mean the vintage Disneyana market will fold. On the contrary, as prices in the past 10 years have seen some wild fluctuations, new collectors have been drawn into the market to scoop up the occasional bargain, and this has caused increased collector interest. With the popularity of Disney films, Disney theme parks, the Disney Channel, and now two hit shows on Broadway, *Beauty and The Beast* and *The Lion King*, Disney character toy collecting has never looked better! It's a great time in collecting history to be a Disneyana collector.

Novices in this field will want to note the distinction between eras of Disneyana merchandising. Most of the very early Mickey Mouse items may have the simple markings "Walter E. Disney" since these items were copyrighted and sold before Kaymen's merchandising phenomenon really kicked in. By the middle 1930s, the establishment of Walt Disney Enterprises clues collectors that these items are 1930s vintage toys, books, or figures manufactured up through 1939 until the release of the very last 1930s feature film, *Pinocchio*. With the advent of *Pinocchio* in 1939, most toys make a switch in markings to bear the copyright of Walt Disney Productions. This company name would last well into the 1980s until toys would start to bear The Walt Disney Company brand. And it has been noted of late that toys in the mid to late 1990s may now once again bear only the mark "Walt Disney." If that's not enough to confuse the new collector, bear in mind that the best key to learning the age of Disney toys is to know the look of the characters at each decade and understand which toy manufacturers were producing Disney toys at the time.

Fisher-Price Disney toys of the 1930s look very different from Fisher-Price Disney toys of the 1940s and the 1950s. Even a novice collector can quickly spot the differences. Mickey and Minnie Mouse of the 1930s have what collectors call "pie-eyes," that is, their eyes look like little black oval pies with one piece cut out. By the late 1930s, the ovals become solid, and by the early 1940s, the Disney characters were drawn with more realistic looking eyes with irises and pupils. The early Donald Duck, introduced in 1935, began with a very "long-billed" almost goose-like beak which was shortened by 1940 to look very much like it does today.

The best advice to collecting fans of Mickey, Minnie, Donald, Pluto and the rest of the gang is to go after what you really like. There is so much available to today's animated cartoon character collector, especially those with a fondness for Disneyana, that it really is up to the individual collector to decide where he or she will specialize.

And from this author who has been a Disney collector for almost 25 years, that is the key word...specialize. Do it now, or do it later, but eventually you will have to get specific about your wants and your likes. If a collector doesn't, the toys themselves may become the master of the house, and children and parents alike may find there is no room in the garage for a car, and no place in the basement for a ping pong table.

Disneyana collectors can pile up collectibles quickly. Use this introductory chapter to Disneyana collectibles to find what you like about vintage cartoon characters and then be selective. It's better to have a couple hundred Disney toys you really love than it is to have a trailer load in your basement that you can't even walk around.

Be selective. Specialize. Demand collector quality condition for all that you buy. Ten years from now, you may thank me. And your Disney cartoon character collection will be a source of great pride.

Mickey Mouse Funny Facts Electric Quiz Game, ©Walt Disney Enterprises, 1930s, rare, found complete, $700.00 – 1,000.00.

Mickey Mouse Funny Facts Electric Quiz Game showing original game cards, terminals, and light-up bulb inside.

Mickey Mouse early German china salt, pepper, and sugar bowl set. Very rare and marked "Germany" on base, $1,800.00 – 2,500.00.

Mickey Mouse and Pluto Drummer Pull Toy by Fisher-Price, ©Walt Disney Ent., 1930s, $800.00 – 1,250.00.

Mickey Mouse Lunch Box. This is the "Grand Daddy" of all great character lunch pails. ©Walt Disney Enterprises, 1930s by Guder, Paeschke, and Frey, $2,000.00 – 3,000.00.

Side view of Mickey Mouse 1930s Lunch Box.

Mickey Mouse Rocking Horse Wood and Celluloid Wind-up, Japan, ©Walt Disney, 1930s. Rare, $3,000.00 – $4,500.00.

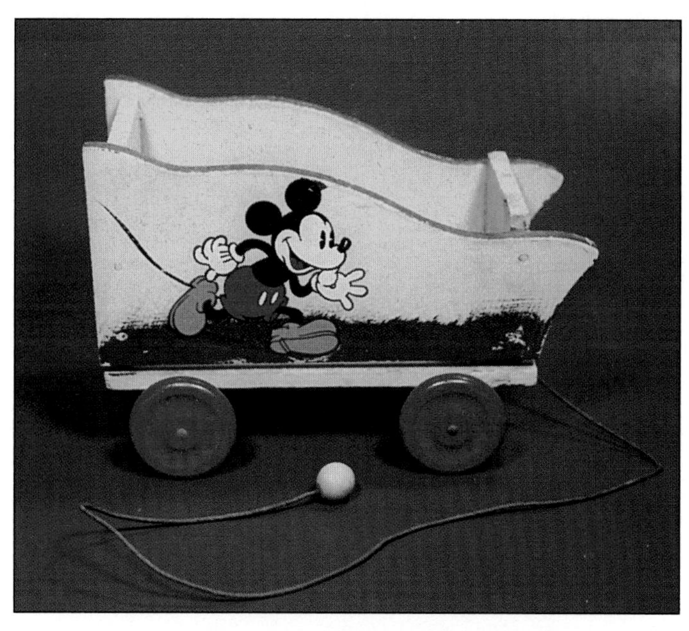

Mickey Mouse Child's Wooden Pull Toy by the Toy Kraft Studios, ©Walt Disney Enterprises, 1930s, $250.00 – 400.00.

Mickey Mouse Whirling Celluloid Wind-up, shown with very rare original box, Japan, ©Walter E. Disney, 1930s, $3,500.00 – 5,000.00.

Mickey Mouse "Tiddleywinks" Game manufactured by Chad Valley of England, 1930s. These feature strikingly colorful graphics, $400.00 – 650.00.

Mickey Mouse Washing Machine with unusual attached wringer, ©Walt Disney Ent., manufactured by Ohio Art, 1930s, $600.00 – 900.00. Front of toy shown above, reverse is shown below.

Mickey Mouse Ingersoll Watch in original box, ©Walt Disney Ent., 1930s, $650.00 – 900.00.

Mickey Mouse Sand Sifter by the Ohio Art Co., 1930s, $250.00 – 400.00.

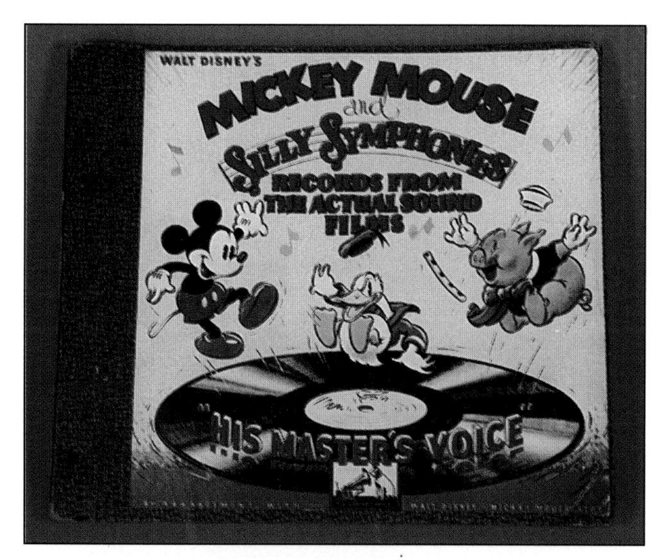

Mickey Mouse "Silly Symphonies" recording by RCA, ©Walt Disney's Mickey Mouse, LTD, from England, 1930s, $250.00 – 375.00.

Mickey Mouse Tea Set in original box by Ohio Art, ©Walt Disney Ent., $400.00 – 550.00.

Mickey Mouse Tambourine by Noble and Cooley, ©Walt Disney Ent., 1930s, $250.00 – 400.00.

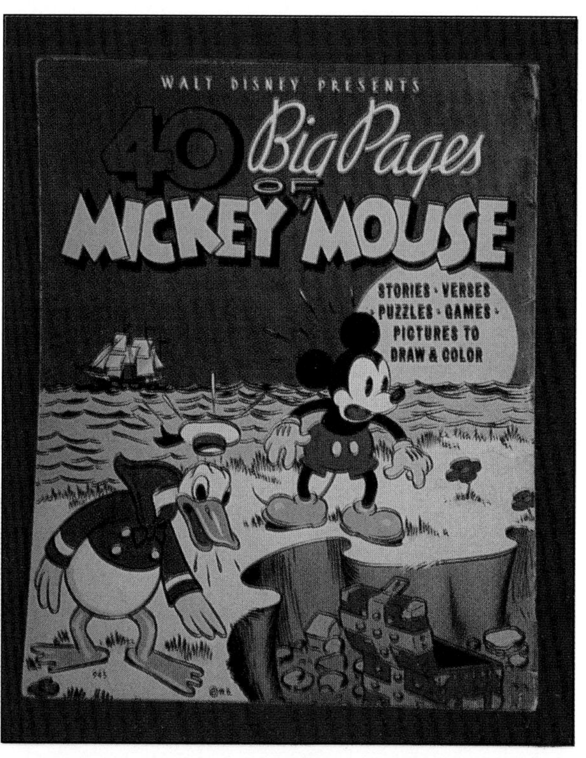

Walt Disney presents 40 Big Pages of Mickey Mouse Story and Activity Book, 1930s, $200.00 – 325.00.

Mickey Mouse Hoop-La Game by Marks Brothers of Boston, ©Walt Disney, 1930s, $350.00 – 500.00.

Mickey Mouse 9" Velvet Doll by Steiff of Germany, ©Walt Disney, 1930s, $950.00 – 1,400.00.

Mickey Mouse and Pluto Plate by Salem China, ©Walt Disney Enterprises, 1930s, $125.00 – 175.00.

Mickey Mouse Party Horn, manufactured by Marks Brothers of Boston, ©Walt Disney, 1930s, $95.00 – 150.00.

Mickey Mouse Flashlight with superb character lithography by USA Light Corp., ©Walt Disney Enterprises, 1930s, $275.00 – 400.00.

Mickey and Pluto 5½" Bisque Figure, ©Walt E. Disney, Japan, circa 1930s, $700.00 – 900.00.

Mickey Mouse Battery-operated Night Light by Micro-Lite, ©Walt Disney Enterprises, 1930s, with tin litho scene of Mickey and Donald around light cylinder, $350.00 – 500.00.

Mickey Mouse Hankies, boxed set, ©Walt Disney Enterprises, 1930s, $325.00 – 400.00.

Mickey and Minnie Mouse Gondoliers Sand Pail by Ohio Art, ©Walt Disney, 1930s. A rare sand pail version, $550.00 – 800.00.

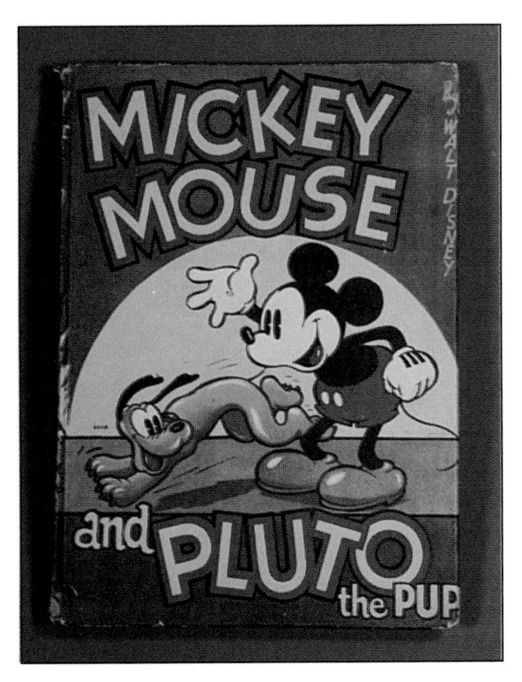

Mickey Mouse and Pluto the Pup by Walt Disney Story Book, ©Walt Disney, 1930s, $200.00 – 350.00.

Mickey Mouse Celluloid Nodder Wind-up, made in Japan, 1930s, $950.00 – 1,400.00.

Mickey Mouse Paperback Storybook, ©Walt Disney, 1930s, $125.00 – 200.00.

Mickey Mouse Metal Cast Detailed Figure, with umbrella, 1930s, $400.00 – 750.00.

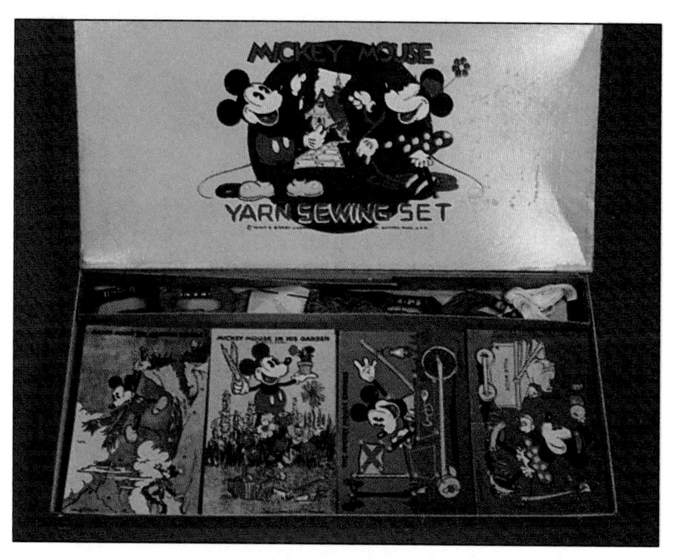

Mickey Mouse Yarn Sewing Set by Marks Brothers of Boston, 1930s, showing colorful original sewing cards. Rare set, $475.00 – 650.00.

Mickey Mouse Bean Bag Game, manufactured by Marks Brothers of Boston, ©Walt Disney Ent., 1930s, $300.00 – 400.00.

Mickey Mouse Scatter Ball Game by Marks Brothers of Boston, 1930s. Strikingly colorful design and graphics, $400.00 – 600.00.

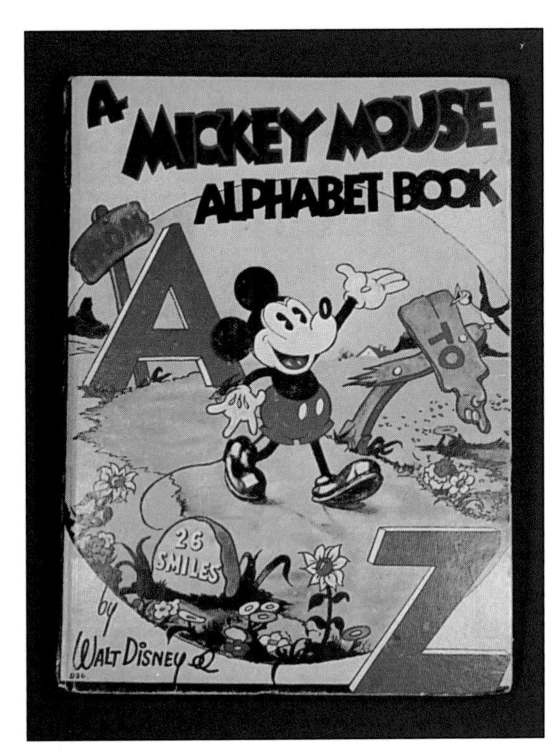

Mickey Mouse Alphabet Book A to Z, ©Walt Disney, 1930s, $150.00 – 275.00.

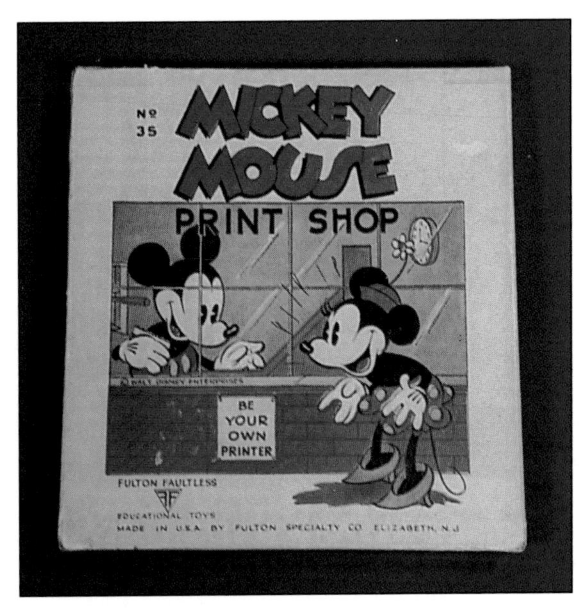

Mickey Mouse Print Shop No. 35 by Fulton Faultless, ©Walt Disney Enterprises, 1930s, $150.00 – 275.00.

Mickey Mouse Large 12" Diameter Drum by Ohio Art, 1930s, $350.00 – 500.00.

Reverse of Drum in photo above.

Mickey Mouse Characters Tin Drum by Ohio Art, ©Walt Disney Ent., 1930s. This drum is an unusual Ohio Art example in that the heads of the drum are not tin, but are made of paper, $325.00 – 475.00.

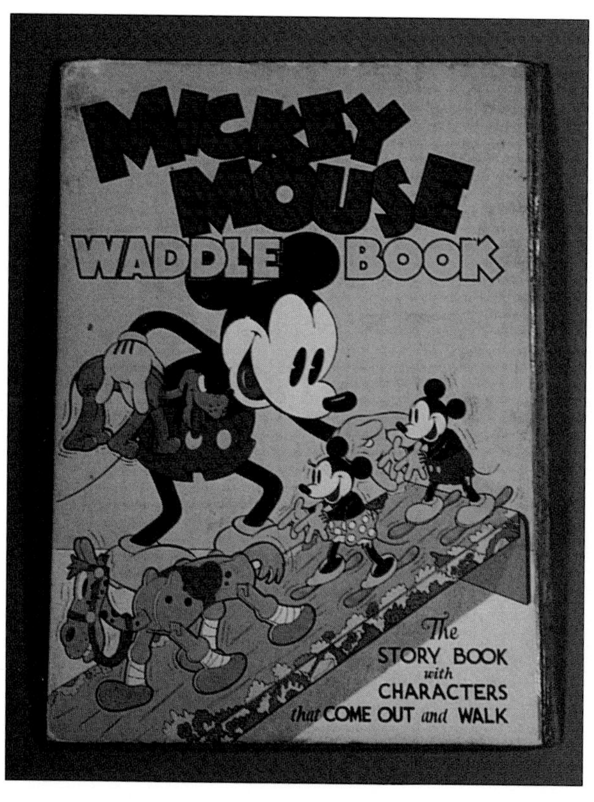

Mickey Mouse Waddle Book published by Blue Ribbon Books, ©Walt Disney, 1930s. Value of book alone is $200.00 – 350.00. Book value complete with Waddles, $1,800.00 – 2,400.00.

"Mickey's Garden" Sand Pail by Ohio Art, ©Walt Disney Enterprises, 1930s, $350.00 – 575.00.

Mickey Mouse Watering Can by Ohio Art, ©Walt Disney Ent., 1930s, $275.00 – 400.00.

Mickey Mouse Watering Can by Ohio Art, Walt Disney Enterprises, 1930s, $300.00 – 475.00.

Mickey Mouse Tin Drum by Ohio Art Co. of Bryan Ohio, 1930s, $250.00 – 400.00.

The Walt Disney Paint Book, ©Walt Disney Enterprises, 1930s. Featuring Giant Coloring Book color pages, $135.00 – 200.00.

Mickey and Minnie Mouse Tin Litho Tea Tray, 1930s, probably French, $150.00 – 22500.

Mickey and Minnie Mouse Tea Tray by Ohio Art, Walt Disney, 1934, $125.00 – 200.00.

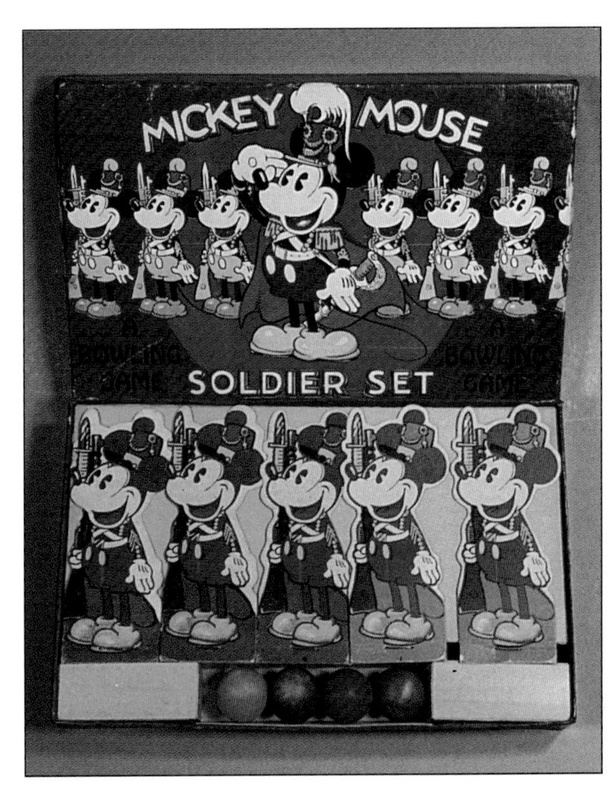

Mickey Mouse Soldier Set Bowling Game in original box, by Marks Brothers of Boston and ©Walt Disney Enterprises, $350.00 – 500.00.

Mickey Mouse Printing Outfit, ©Walt Disney Mickey Mouse, LTD. Made in England, 1930s, $200.00 – 350.00.

Mickey Mouse small store display or premium for Dixon Pencil Boxes, Walt Disney, 1930s, $75.00 – 100.00.

Mickey Mouse, The Mail Pilot Big Little Book, Walt Disney, 1930s, $40.00 – 65.00.

Mickey Mouse Bayard French Alarm Clock, 1930s. Shown with extremely rare original box, $950.00 – 1,200.00.

Mickey Mouse Safety Film by Keystone Manufacturing Co. of Boston, Mass. ©Walt Disney Ent., $75.00 – 125.00.

Mickey Mouse Cowboy Doll by Knickerbocker, shown with original accessories and wrist tag, 1930s. Rare, $3,000.00 – 4,500.00.

Circus Dining Car for the Mickey Mouse Circus Train, Walt Disney Ent., 1930s, $400.00 – 650.00.

Lionel's "Commodore Vanderbilt" Wind-up Engine which powers the Mickey Mouse Circus Train Engine, 1930s, $150.00 – 275.00.

Mickey Mouse Band Train Car for the Mickey Mouse Circus Train, ©Walt Disney Ent., $400.00 – 650.00.

Lionel Mickey Mouse Stoker Car for the Mickey Mouse Circus Train, 1930s, $300.00 – 500.00.

Mickey Mouse Circus Train Car for Lionel Circus Train Set, ©Walt Disney Ent., 1930s, $400.00 – 650.00. Value for complete Train Set, $3,000.00 – 5,000.00.

Mickey Mouse Tin Lithographed Top, ©Walt Disney 1930s, $325.00 – 500.00.

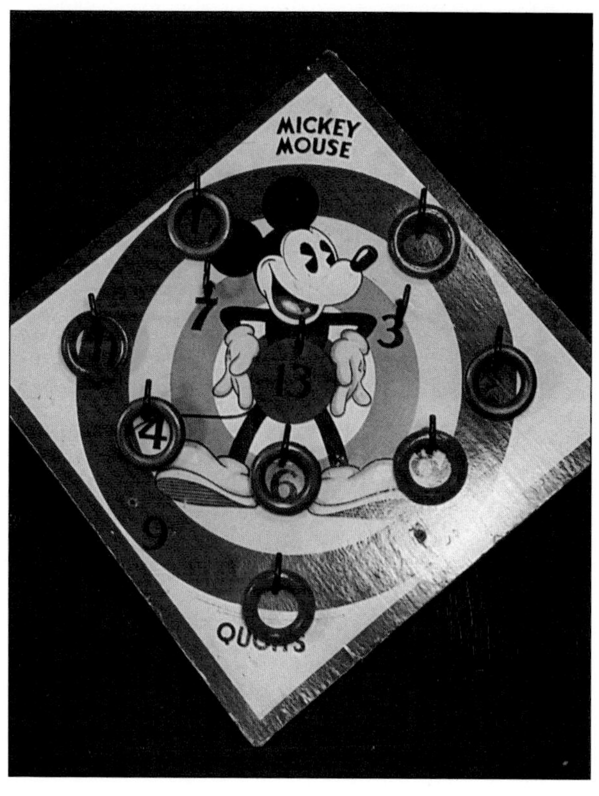

Mickey Mouse Quoits Ring Toss Game, by Chad Valley of England, 1930s, $250.00 – 350.00.

Mickey Mouse ABC Story Book by Walt Disney, 1930s, $150.00 – 275.00.

Mickey Mouse and Donald Duck Tin, European, 1930s. Note the unusual addition of a T.V. for a piece this early, $650.00 – 1,000.00.

Mickey Mouse Pull Toy by N.N. Hill Brass, ©Walt Disney Enterprises, 1930s, $450.00 – 750.00.

Mickey Mouse Pencil Tablet, manufactured by Powers Paper as a child's standard school tablet. ©Walt Disney Enterprises, 1930s, $85.00 – 135.00.

Mickey Mouse Large Wood Jointed Fun-e-Flex Doll with original ears and solid wood head. Original decal on chest spells "Mickey." ©Walt Disney, 1930s, $850.00 – 1,200.00.

Mickey Mouse and Pluto Bisque Toothbrush Holder, 1930s. Made in Japan, $275.00 – 450.00.

Mickey Mouse Drum Major Giant 15" Doll by Knickerbocker, 1930s, $1,200.00 – 1,700.00.

Mickey Mouse Felt Doll with original clothes and mother-of-pearl buttons, circa 1930s, $600.00 – 850.00.

Minnie Mouse Felt Doll with original clothes, circa 1930s, $600.00 – 850.00.

Mickey Mouse Sand Pail by Ohio Art, Walt Disney Enterprises, 1930s, $350.00 – 550.00.

Mickey Mouse Composition Bank, by Crown Toy and Novelty, ©Walt Disney Ent., 1930s, $400.00 – 575.00.

Mickey Mouse in King Arthur's Court with pop-up illustrations, ©Walt Disney Enterprises, 1930s. Features beautiful 3-D pop-ups throughout and is shown with rarely found dust jacket, $350.00 – 550.00.

Illustration of one pop-up in the Mickey Mouse in King Arthur's Court Book.

Detail of illustration of pop-up Mickey figure inside the Mickey Mouse in King Arthur's Court Book.

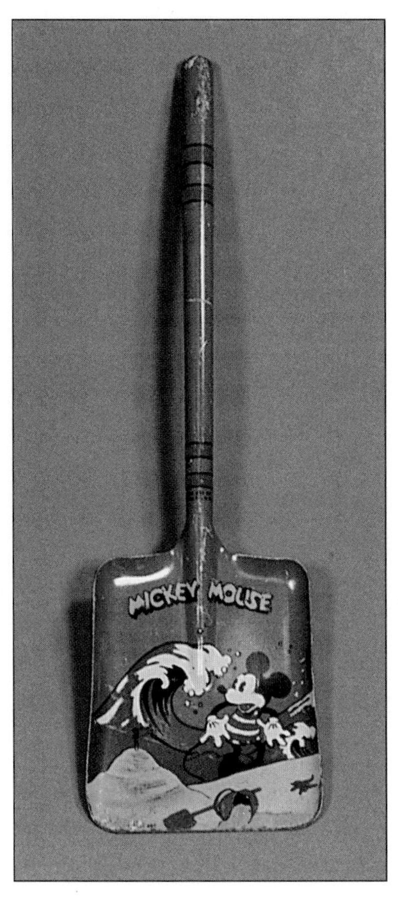

Large Mickey Mouse Sand Shovel by Ohio Art, ©Walt Disney Enterprises, 1930s, $150.00 – 250.00.

Mickey Mouse Book No. 4 Picture Storybook published by the David McKay Company Publishers of Philadelphia, 1930s, $200.00 – 400.00.

Mickey Mouse Top, 1930s. Distributed by George Borgfeldt and featuring all the early Disney characters. Makes musical tones when spinning, $350.00 – 600.00.

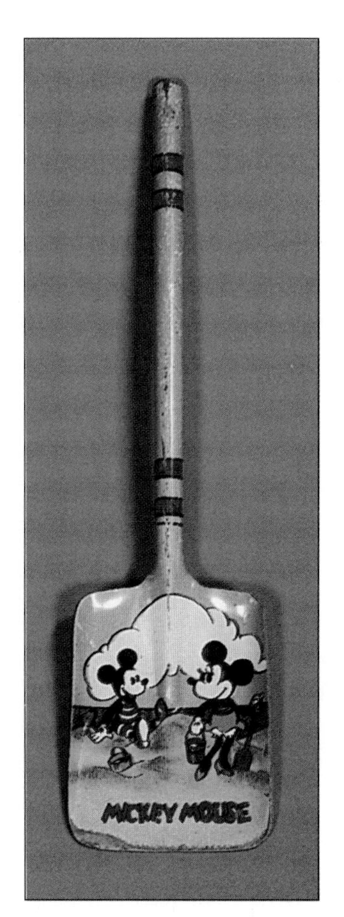

Mickey and Minnie Mouse Sand Shovel by Ohio Art, ©Walt Disney Enterprises, 1930s, $125.00 – 250.00.

Mickey and Minnie Mouse Sand Pail by Ohio Art, 1930s, $400.00 – 650.00.

Mickey Mouse Sand Pail by Ohio Art, ©Walt Disney enterprises, 1930s. Scene of Mickey fishing while he daydreams watching Minnie on the shore, $600.00 – 900.00.

Mickey Mouse Pail by Ohio Art, ©Walt Disney Enterprises, 1930s. Features 1930s Disney Characters on all sides, $400.00 – 650.00.

Long-billed Donald Duck Pull Toy by Fisher-Price Toys, 1930s. Toy makes a quacking sound when pulled along, $400.00 – 700.00.

Mickey Mouse Safety Blocks, manufactured by Halsam, ©Walt Disney Enterprises, $150.00 – 250.00.

Giant Mickey Mouse Sand Pail by Ohio Art, 1930s. The large size makes this a particularly desirable design, $700.00 – 1,000.00.

Mickey Mouse Halsam Blocks with box open showing mint condition. 20-block set, 1930s, $150.00 – 250.00.

Mickey Mouse Fishing Scene Sand Pail by Ohio Art of Bryan, Ohio, 1930s, $600.00 – 1,000.00.

Mickey Mouse 6" Sand Pail by Ohio Art, 1930s. Pictures Mickey and Minnie building a sand castle, $275.00 – 500.00.

Mickey Mouse Windup Celluloid Whirly-gig Toy, ©Walt Disney and Made in Japan, 1930s, $1,800.00 – 2,500.00.

Mickey Mouse Ingersoll Watch Box, ©Walt Disney Enterprises, 1930s. Unusual hat and cane version of Mickey makes this a particularly desirable box. Value is for box only, $150.00 – 300.00.

Mickey Mouse Mazda Lights, showing interior box flap, lights, and lamp covers. ©Walt Disney Mickey Mouse, LTD., 1930s. Made in England, $400.00 – 700.00.

Mickey Mouse Piano by Marks Brothers of Boston, ©Walt Disney Enterprises, 1930s, $1,800.00 – 3,000.00.

Mickey and Minnie Mouse Lionel Hand Car, ©Walt Disney Ent., 1930s, $900.00 – 1,200.00.

Mickey Mouse Target Set by Marks Brothers of Boston, ©Walt Disney Ent., 1930s, boxed value set, $300.00 – 500.00.

Mickey Mouse Pop Game Target Set by Marks Brothers of Boston, Walt Disney Enterprises, 1930s, $300.00 – 500.00.

Giant Mickey Mouse George Borgfeldt Distributors Top, 14" in diameter. The largest of all Disney tops. ©Walt Disney Enterprises, 1930s. Very rare, $750.00 – 1,000.00.

Mickey Mouse Tin Sand Pail by Happynak of England, ©Walt Disney Mickey Mouse, LTD, 1930s. Rare, $750.00 – 950.00.

Side view of Pail shown above. One of the rare Disney pails where a long-billed Donald Duck is shown.

Donald Duck Back-up by Fisher-Price, C.W.D. Ent. Extremely rare Fisher-Price windup toy that walks backwards, $1,800.00 – 3,000.00.

Mickey Mouse Ludo Game by Chad Valley of England, 1930s, $350.00 – 475.00.

Game Board for Ludo. Game pictured above.

Pluto Fisher-Price Toy, ©Walt Disney Ent., 1930s, $275.00 – 350.00.

Mickey Mouse Bell Bread Labels, ©Walt Disney from 1930s series, $15.00 – 25.00 each.

Donald Duck and Pluto Cart Pull Toy by Fisher-Price, ©Walt Disney Ent. Very rare, $2,000.00 – 3,000.00.

Mickey Mouse Bell Bread Labels, 1930s, $15.00 – 25.00 each.

Mickey Mouse Fisher-Price Toy, ©Walt Disney Ent., 1930s, $300.00 – 450.00.

Mickey Mouse Bell Bread Labels, ©Walt Disney, 1930s, $15.00 – 25.00 each.

Mickey Mouse Bell Bread Labels, ©Walt Disney, 1930s, $15.00 – 25.00 each.

Bell Bread Co. Mickey Mouse Recipe Scrap Book, ©Walt Disney, 1930s, $75.00 – 125.00.

Mickey Mouse Bell Recipe Book Bread Labels, ©Walt Disney, 1930s, $15.00 – 25.00 each.

Mickey Mouse Wooden Brush, ©Walt Disney Ent., 1930s, manufactured by Hughes, $30.00 – 45.00.

Mickey Mouse Boxed Brush Set by Hughes Autograph, ©Walt Disney Ent., 1930s, $300.00 – 450.00.

Goofy Mechanical Wind-up Toy by Line Mar, ©Walt Disney Productions. Shown with original box, $550.00 – 750.00.

Mickey and Pluto Tiny 3" Sand Pail. Pictures Mickey fishing on dock. Extremely rare design by Ohio Art, $400.00 – 650.00.

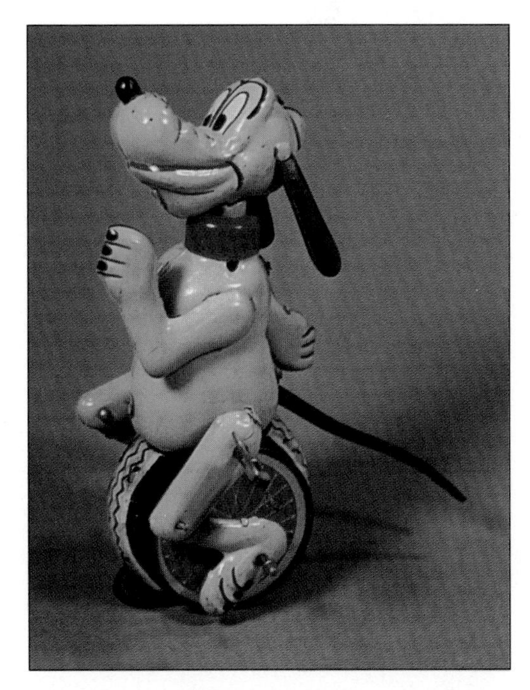

Pluto Unicyclist Tin Wind-up Toy by Line Mar, Japan, ©Walt Disney Productions, 1960s, $650.00 – 825.00.

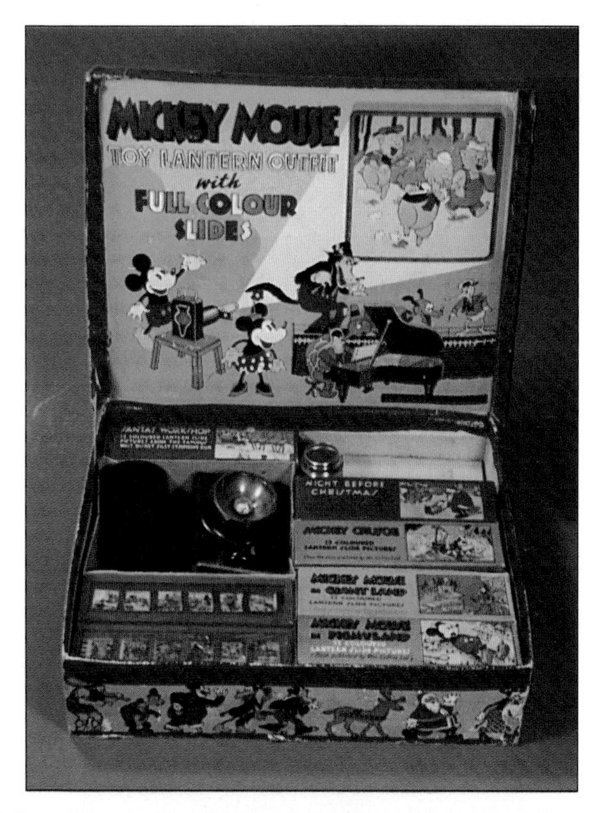

Mickey Mouse Toy Lantern Outfit, copyrighted by Walt Disney's Mickey Mouse, LTD. from England, 1930s. Contains battery-powered lantern and packages of slides for viewing, $500.00 – 750.00.

Mickey Mouse Post Toasties Box, 1930s. Unusual to find boxes complete. This one features a highly collectible design of Mickey as a G-man, $150.00 – 275.00.

Mickey Mouse Tall Party Horn by Marks Brothers of Boston, Mass., ©Walt Disney, 1930s. Unusual very long, tall version, $150.00 – 275.00.

Mickey Mouse Lusterware Perfume Bottle with Art Deco styling, circa 1930s. Very desirable ceramic Disney piece, $650.00 – 950.00.

The "Pop-up" Mickey Mouse in Ye Olden Days Picture Book, by Blue Ribbon Books, 1930s, $150.00 – 275.00.

Mickey Mouse on Cart Riding Toy by Steiff, 1930s. Very rare, $2,500.00 – 3,500.00.

Mickey Mouse Picture Printing Set, ©Walt Disney Ent., by Fulton Specialty Co., 1930s, $275.00 – 400.00.

Donald Duck Bank by Crown Toy and Novelty, C.W.D. Ent., 1930s, $400.00 – 600.00.

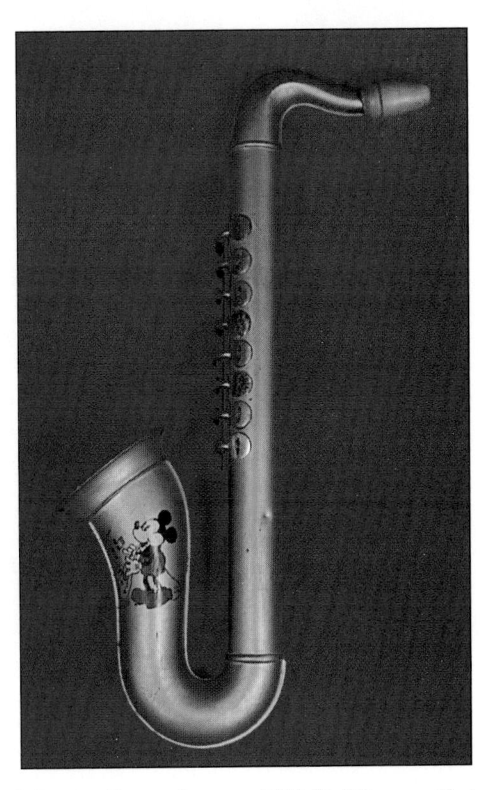

Mickey Mouse Saxophone, ©Walt Disney Ent., 1930s, $400.00 – 650.00.

Mickey and Minnie Mouse Bisque Toothbrush Holder Figures with movable arms, ©Walt Disney, 1930s, Japan, $350.00 – 500.00 each.

Mickey and Minnie Mouse Celluloid Figures, ©Walt Disney, 1930s, $300.00 – 500.00 each.

Mickey Mouse Wood and Composition Doll with Mickey decal on chest, Walt Disney Ent., 1930s, $1,200.00 – 1,800.00.

Donald Duck, 4½" Bisque Figure, 1930s, $400.00 – 500.00.
Mickey Mouse, 6½" Bisque Figure. Rare, $450.00 – 750.00.

Mickey Mouse Small Fisher-Price Toy from the Carnival Set, ©W.D. Ent., 1930s, $275.00 – 400.00.

Elmer the Elephant, small Fisher-Price Toy, ©W.D. Ent., from the Carnival Set, $250.00 – 350.00.

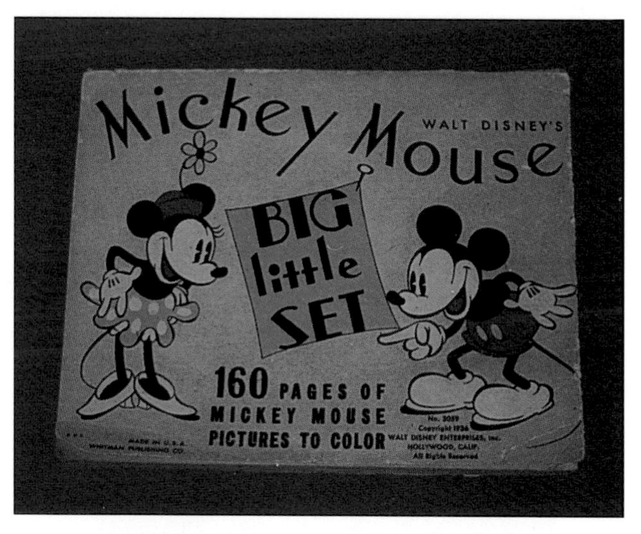

Mickey Mouse Big Little Set of Coloring Pictures, ©W.D. Ent., 1930s, $75.00 – 100.00.

Pluto, small Fisher-Price Rolling Figure, ©W.D. Ent., from the Carnival Set, 1930s, $275.00 – 400.00.

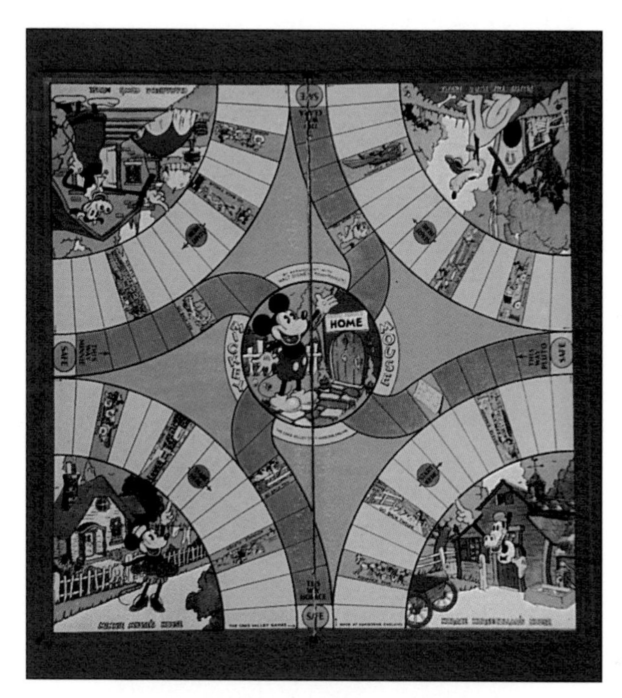

Mickey Mouse Coming Home Board Game, 1930s, unusual English version of Board by Chad Valley of England, $150.00 – 200.00.

Donald Duck, small Fisher-Price Figure from the Carnival Set, ©W.D. Ent., 1930s, $275.00 – 400.00.

Long-billed Donald Duck Fisher-Price Push Toy, ©Walt Disney Ent., 7" tall, 1930s, $300.00 – 400.00.

Mickey Mouse Wood Composition Doll by Knickerbocker Toy, 1930s. Doll has movable head and arms and is highly prized by vintage Disney collectors, $900.00 – 1,200.00.

Long-billed Donald Duck Doll by Knickerbocker, 1930s. Doll features movable head and legs and is made of wood composition, $700.00 – 1,000.00.

Mazda Mickey Mouse Lights Set by The British Thomson Houston Co., 1930s. Box inside and out is profusely illustrated with colorful decal decorated lamp covers, $400.00 – 700.00.

Mickey Mouse Mechanical Racing Car, ©Walt Disney Enterprises, 1930s. Unusual to find with original box, $750.00 – 950.00.

Mickey Mouse Tin Lithographic Sand Sifter by Ohio Art,. ©Walt Disney Enterprises, 1930s, $175.00 – 275.00.

Mickey the Driver Tin Windup Car by Marks. ©Walt Disney Productions, 1950s. Shown with original box, $650.00 – 950.00.

Mickey and Minnie Mouse Bisque Toothbrush Holder, ©Walt E. Disney, Japan, 1930s, $250.00 – 400.00.

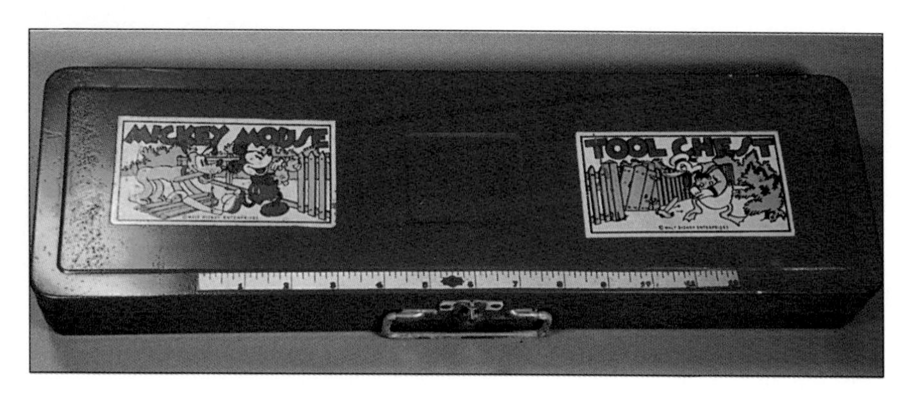

Mickey Mouse Metal Tool Chest, ©Walt Disney Enterprises, 1930s, $175.00 – 300.00.

Mickey Mouse Figural Soap in colorful box, ©Walt Disney Enterprises, 1930s, $150.00 – 300.00.

Mickey and Minnie Mouse Celluloid Wind-up Acrobat Toy, made in Japan, circa 1930s, $900.00 – 1,500.00.

Mickey Mouse Coming Home Game Box, which holds small game pieces, 1930s, $125.00 – 200.00.

"The Mad Hatter Sky-view Taxi," friction toy with siren by Line Mar of Japan, ©Walt Disney Productions. Shown with original box, $400.00 – 650.00.

Donald Duck 6" Celluloid Wind-up Toy, Japan, ©Walt Disney, 1930s, $1,000.00 – 1,400.00.

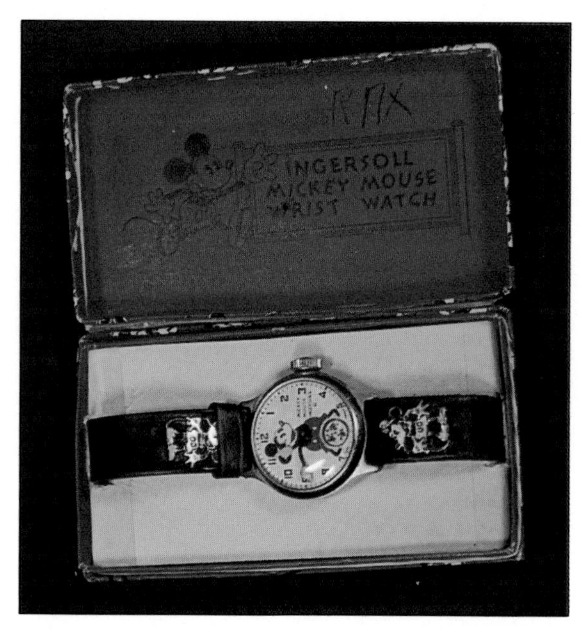

Ingersoll Mickey Mouse Wrist Watch, 1930s. In original box with leather watch band shown, $500.00 – 750.00.

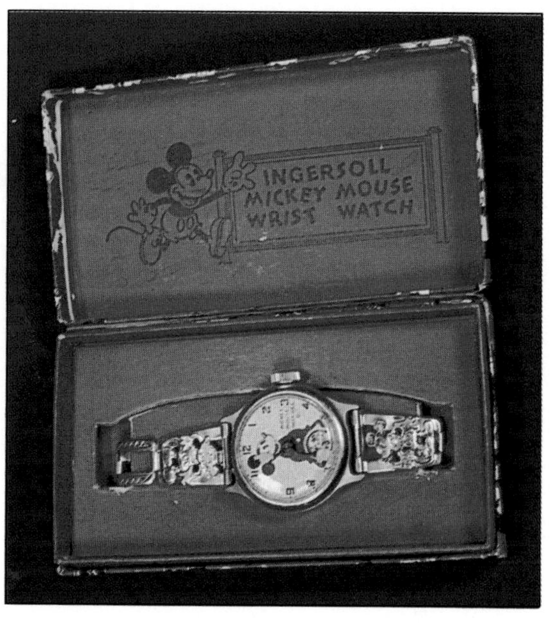

Mickey Mouse Ingersoll Watch with metal band in original 1930s box, $500.00 – 700.00.

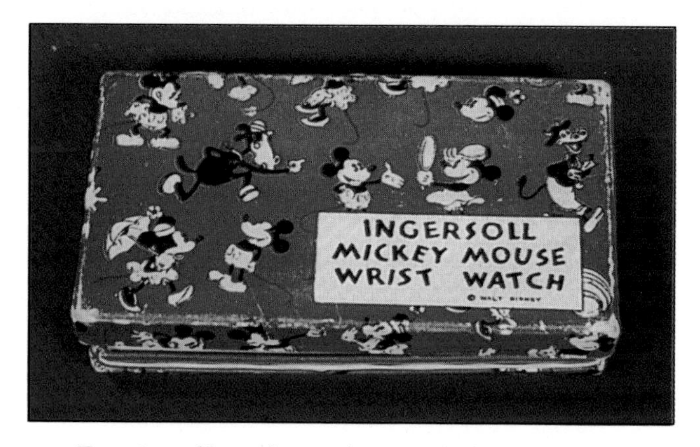

Exterior of box shown for watch shown above.

Mickey Mouse Chocolate Bar, original box by Paterson, 1930s. Rare, $150.00 – 275.00.

Mickey and Minnie Mouse Lusterware Glazed China Ashtray, Walt Disney Enterprises, 1930s, $250.00 – 400.00.

Mickey Mouse Sparkler Toy, by Nifty and distributed by George Borgfeldt and Co., 1930s. Rare with box, $1,000.00 – 1,500.00.

Mickey Mouse Tin Drum by Ohio Art, ©Walt Disney Ent., 1930s, $200.00 – 375.00.

Mickey Mouse Large 12" Diameter Drum by Ohio Art, ©W.D. Ent., 1930s, $300.00 – 450.00.

Mickey Mouse Trapeze Wind-up Celluloid Toy, ©Walt E. Disney, 1930s. Unusual, very small, 5". Toy size is rare. Japan. With original box, $700.00 – 950.00.

Other side of Drum pictured in above photo.

The Story of Mickey Mouse, The Big Big Book, ©Walt Disney Enterprises, 1930s, $125.00 – 175.00.

Mickey Mouse Stuffed Velvet and Satin Doll by Charlotte Clark. Rare, early 1930s, $1,500.00 – 2,000.00.

More Adventures of Mickey Mouse, ©Walt Disney Ent., 1930s, $100.00 – 150.00.

Mickey Mouse Doll by Knickerbocker with wood composition shoes, ©Walt Disney, 1930s, $550.00 – 800.00.

Mickey Mouse Tin Tea Set Tray by Ohio Art, ©Walt Disney Enterprises, 1930s, $150.00 – 250.00.

Mickey Mouse Tool Chest by Climax, ©Walt Disney Enterprises, 1930s. Top view, $450.00 – 700.00.

Mickey Mouse Tool Chest, side front view.

Mickey Mouse Coloring Book with die-cut cover and inside pages, 1930s, ©W.D. Ent., $150.00 – 200.00.

Donald Duck and Mickey Mouse Solid Filled Celluloid Figures, Walt Disney, 1930s. Rare versions, $200.00 – 350.00 each.

Mickey Mouse Ingersoll Watch with original leather strap and watch fob, 1930s, $400.00 – 650.00.

Minnie Mouse 6" Jointed Arms and Head Poseable Celluloid Toy, Japan, ©Walt Disney, 1930s, $750.00 – 950.00.

Donald Duck Walt Disney Picture Story Book by Whitman, ©Walt Disney Enterprises, 1930s, $65.00 – 95.00.

Mickey Mouse Toothpick Holder by S. Maw and Sons of England, 1930s, $750.00 – 1,000.00.

Minnie Mouse Toothpick Holder by S. Maw and Sons of England, 1930s, marked "Genuine Copyright – Foreign" on base, $850.00 – 1,100.00.

Mickey Mouse "Let them all come" Ring Toss Game by Chad Valley of England, Mickey Mouse, LTD., ©Walt Disney, 1930s, $400.00 – 650.00.

Mickey Mouse Toilet Soap, boxed set, 1930s. Featuring decals that outlasted the soap. Unusual set, $150.00 – 225.00.

Mickey Mouse Tin Tea Set Tray by Ohio Art, ©Walt Disney Ent., circa 1930s, $175.00 – 275.00.

Reverse of Mickey Soap box pictured above.

Early Mickey Mouse Art Deco Style French Creamer, ©Walt Disney, 1930s. Pictures Minnie Mouse on reverse, $325.00 – 475.00.

Mickey Mouse Tin Sand Pail by Ohio Art, ©Walt Disney Enterprises, 1930s. Showing Mickey running a lemonade stand, $250.00 – 375.00.

Mickey Mouse Tin Sea Saucer, probably French, 1930s, "Par authorization Walt Disney," $50.00 – 75.00.

Mickey Mouse Celluloid Rolatoy, ©Walt Disney, 1930s. With chiming rattle inside, $175.00 – 300.00.

Mickey Mouse Wooden Hat Stand, ©Walt Disney Enterprises, 1930s, $300.00 – 400.00.

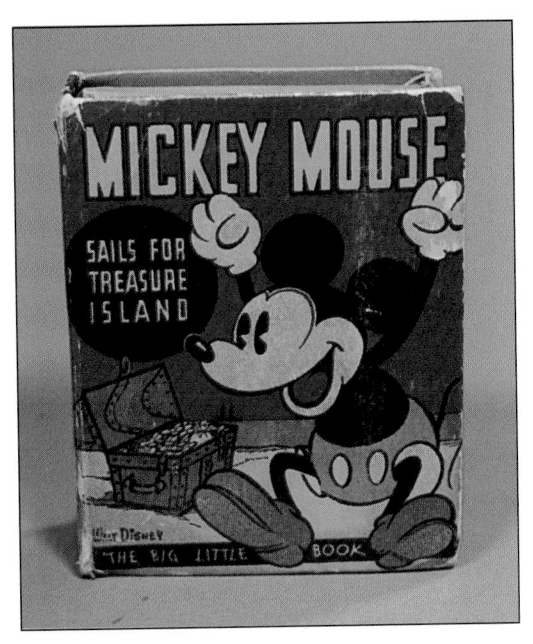

"Mickey Mouse Sails for Treasure Island," Big Little Book, ©Walt Disney, 1930s, $50.00 – 75.00.

Mickey Mouse Bagatelle Game by Walt Disney Mickey Mouse, LTD., Chad Valley of England, 1930s, $800.00 – 1,100.00.

Rare 10" Mickey and Minnie Mouse Old Jalopy Sand Pail, giant size. One of the rarest of all Ohio Art Disney Sand Pails, $1,500.00 – 2,000.00.

Mickey Mouse Tin Sand Pail by Ohio Art, ©Walt Disney Ent., 1930s, $300.00 – 500.00.

Mickey Mouse Composition Figure by Lionel Trains, 1930s, which came with the Mickey Mouse Circus Train Set, $275.00 – 400.00.

Mickey Mouse Circus Game by Marks Brothers of Boston, ©Walt Disney Enterprises. Photo shows inside stand-up marble drop game board. Price for game complete, $650.00 – 900.00.

Mickey Mouse Circus Game pictured above right. Shown here is opened game board.

Mickey Mouse Tin Pail by Ohio Art, ©Walt Disney Ent., 1930s, $250.00 – 400.00.

Mickey Mouse Band Leader, Fisher-Price Toys, Walt Disney Ent., 1930s, $400.00 – 600.00.

Mickey Mouse Drummer Toy by Fisher-Price, ©Walt Disney Enterprises, 1930s. A most desirable early Fisher Price Disney Toy, $550.00 – 825.00.

Donald Duck Art Stamp Picture Set, ©Walt Disney Enterprises. Manufactured by Fulton Specialty Co. of Elizabeth, N.J., 1930s, $175.00 – 300.00.

Donald Duck Tin Sweeper by Ohio Art, ©Walt Disney Enterprises, 1930s, $150.00 – 250.00.

Disney Character large George Borgfeldt Tin Musical Top with colorful lithography, 1930s, $350.00 – 500.00.

Mickey and Minnie Mouse "The Two Pals" Bisque Set, ©Walt E. Disney and Made in Japan. Shown with original box, $550.00 – 900.00.

Mickey Mouse Santa Planter by Leeds China, 1940s. Very rare style, $200.00 – 350.00.

Donald Duck Composition Figure fashioned into a calendar holder, 1930s. This figure also appears on the Lionel Donald Duck Rail Car, $325.00 – 450.00.

Mickey Mouse Composition Book, Walt Disney Enterprises, manufactured by The Powers Paper Co., 1930s, $125.00 – 250.00.

Donald Duck Locomotive, Fisher-Price Toys, ©Walt Disney Ent., 1930s, $350.00 – 500.00.

Pluto Wind-up Lever Action Tail Rolling Toy by Louis Marx, ©Walt Disney Enterprises, 1930s, $225.00 – 375.00.

Donald Duck Pull Toy by Fisher Price, ©Walt Disney Enterprises, 1930s, $450.00 – 750.00.

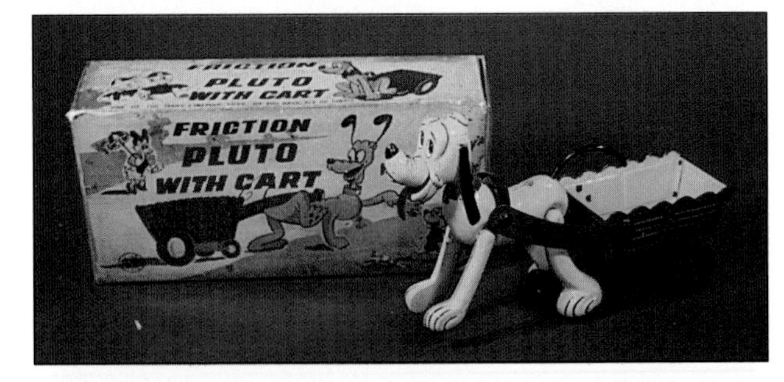

Friction Pluto with Cart, Disney Toy, ©Walt Disney Productions. Manufactured by Line Mar, Japan. Shown with original box. $600.00 – 950.00.

Long-billed Donald Duck Composition Wind-up Toy, ©Walt Disney by George Borgfeldt Dist., 1930s, $1,500.00 – 2,000.00.

Mickey Mouse Dominoes by Halsam, ©Walt Disney Ent., 1930s, $250.00 – 375.00.

Walt Disney's Rocking Chair String Pull Action Tin and Celluloid Toy. Manufactured by Line Mar Toys of Japan. Shown with original box, $600.00 – 850.00.

Ceramic Long-billed Donald Duck Planter, glazed finish, ©Walt Disney, circa 1930s, $350.00 – 475.00.

Lionel Donald Duck Rail Car by Lionel Trains. ©Walt Disney Enterprises, 1930s. Shown with original box, $1,500.00 – 2,200.00.

Mickey Mouse French Vera Puzzle, ©Walt Disney, 1930s, $175.00 – 250.00.

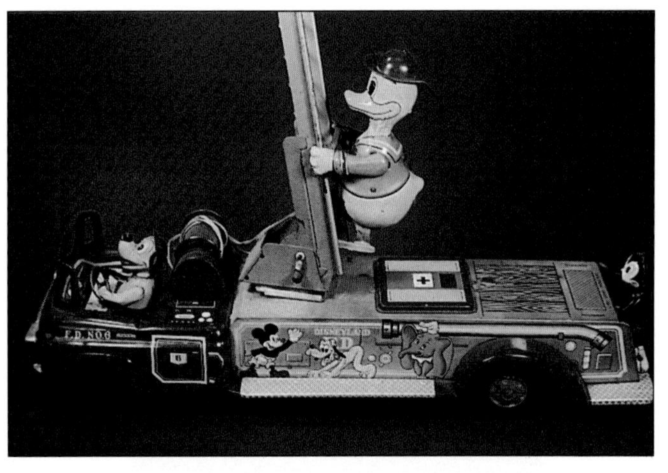

Disney Battery-operated Fire Engine Tin Toy by Line Mar, ©Walt Disney Productions. Action figure of Donald Duck Fireman climbs the ladder, $650.00 – 900.00.

Walt Disney's Easter Parade by Fisher-Price Toys, Inc. ©Walt Disney Enterprises, 1930s. Set of five figures including Donald Duck and Clara Cluck. In original box, $1,000.00 – 1,500.00.

Mechanical Drum Major Pluto Tin Wind-up, ©Walt Disney Prod. by Line Mar of Japan. Shown with original box, $650.00 – 900.00.

Pluto Lantern, ©Walt Disney Prod. by Line Mar Toys, Japan. Shown with original box, $300.00 – 500.00.

Mickey Mouse Riding a Unicycle Wind-up Toy by Line Mar, Japan, ©Walt Disney Productions, $750.00 – 900.00.

Goofy on a Unicycle Wind-up by Line Mar, Japan, ©Walt Disney Productions, $750.00 – 900.00.

Mickey Mouse Figural Plaster Lamp by The Soreng-Manegold Co., Walt Disney Enterprises, 1930s, $1,700.00 – 2,500.00.

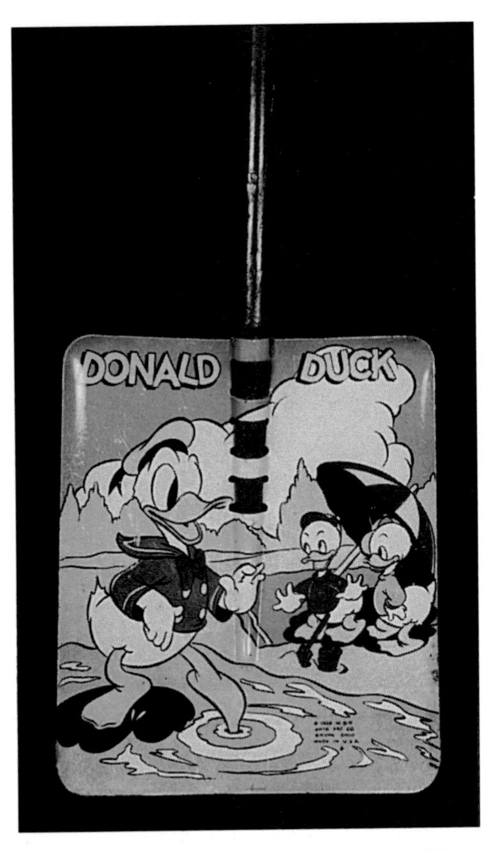

Donald Duck Tin Shovel by Ohio Art Co. of Bryan, Ohio, 1930s, $150.00 – 275.00.

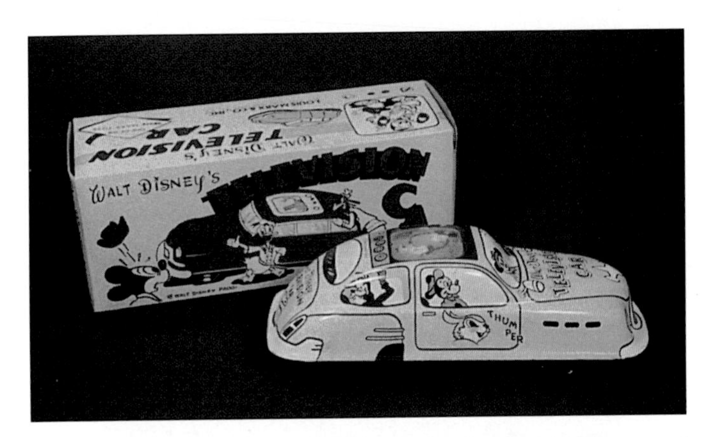

Walt Disney Television Wind-up Car by Louis Marx and Co. Inc., 1950s. Shown with original box, $350.00 – 600.00.

Pluto the Pup Wind-up Rolling Action Toy by Line Mar, Japan, 1960s. Striking colors with excellent wind-up action, $300.00 – 600.00.

Disney Dipsy Car, manufactured by Louis Marx, circa 1950s. Shown with original box, $500.00 – 850.00.

Pluto Gym-Toys Acrobat, ©Walt Disney Productions, 1950s. Manufactured by Line Mar, Japan. Shown with original box, $400.00 – 750.00.

Rare Donald Duck "Dough Boy" Fisher-Price Pull Toy, war time design picturing Pluto pulling Donald dressed as a soldier. Part of artillery cannon (as shown) in example is missing, $350.00 – 600.00.

Mechanical Donald Duck Drummer, ©Walt Disney Productions. Manufactured by Line Mar, $700.00 – 1,000.00.

Donald Duck Bell-ringing Pull Toy by N.N. Hill Brass, ©Walt Disney Enterprises, 1930s, $350.00 – 550.00.

Mickey Mouse and Donald Duck Weather Forecaster, hard plastic child's barometer. Shown with rare original box, $150.00 – 275.00.

Donald Duck Wind-up Line Mar Tricycle with original box, ©Walt Disney Prod., $400.00 – 650.00.

Walt Disney's Mechanical Tricycle by Line Mar, showing Mickey Mouse, ©Walt Disney Prod., 1960s. Shown with original box, $400.00 – 650.00.

Goofy Tin Wind-up Tricycle by Line Mar, ©Walt Disney Productions, $500.00 – 800.00.

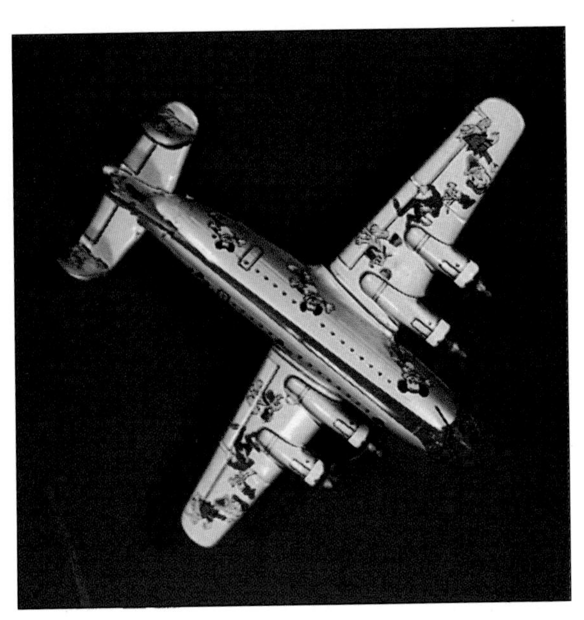

Mickey Mouse Airplane by Line Mar, Japan, ©Walt Disney Prod., $400.00 – 650.00.

Donald Duck Sand Pail by Ohio Art, Walt Disney Productions, 1940s, $250.00 – 400.00.

Mickey Mouse Tin Wind-up by Line Mar, Japan, ©Walt Disney Productions, 1950s, $450.00 – 600.00.

WARNER BROTHERS CARTOON COLLECTIBLES

Although the first chapter of the book has already given extensive coverage to merchandising and popularity of the animated film characters of the Walt Disney Studios, Warner Brothers had its own answer to the popularity of Mickey Mouse. Meet Bugs Bunny.

In some respects, Bugs Bunny is a more pure animated character icon. We're not talking morality or personality here; both Bugs and Mickey have done their share of pranks, tricks, and bratty deeds over the past five decades. But Bugs Bunny has not been over-merchandised in the way that many of the Disney film characters have. Ask any Warner Brothers Looney Tunes collector how easy it is to find all that they are looking for, and they will answer, "It's tough. Really tough."

One of the reasons Bugs has remained less marketed is Warner Brothers has kept him primarily in two media; that is, you can see Bugs on television or at the movies, and that's pretty much it! Whereas Mickey Mouse is seen as a live character personality at the theme parks, a corporate symbol for all that Disney represents, a film, television, cable, Internet, greeting card and general merchandising phenomenon, Bugs Bunny, for the most part, has remained plain old Bugs Bunny. He is exactly what he was and has been for the past 60 years...a fun-to-watch cartoon character.

Leon Schlesinger was responsible for creating the earliest of all Bugs designs in the 1930s, although the popularity of Bugs as a toy, comic book, and merchandise entity didn't really take hold until the 1940s. Warner Brothers character collectors today seek out the very early vintage Bugs, Daffy Duck, Porky Pig, and Elmer Fudd toys drawn in the 1930s – early 1940s style marked simply "©Leon Schlesinger." This marking signals a collector that this is a Looney Tunes collectible from somewhere prior to 1945. Beginning in the mid-1940s, Leon Schlesinger-marked merchandise shows "© Warner Brothers" as it remains up to the present.

Warner Brothers collectors usually can't be quite as specialized as Disneyana enthusiasts simply because they don't have the monumental selection to choose from. For one thing, Bugs Bunny films were used by Warner Brothers simply as film shorts to trail between double features released by that studio, or they were sandwiched as lead-ins to single features somewhere in the middle of the previews. As long as Bugs remained an entertaining animated film character, that was really all that was asked of him. Warner Brothers Studios did not go to the great lengths to merchandise their cartoon characters that the Walt Disney Studios did. Animated films were the flagship of Disney, and they sought every dime that could be made off the characters and their merchandising in the 1930s – 1950s. Certainly Bugs Bunny and Looney Tunes/Merrie Melodies were hits with children on both television and at the movies during those decades, but since Warner Brothers was mainly a live action film studio with plenty of live action film stars to promote, Bugs Bunny got a rather raw deal. He, along with Daffy, Sylvester, Porky Pig, and Elmer Fudd never got the merchandising push that Kay Kaymen gave Walt Disney. Toys were made in the likenesses of Warner Brothers characters and character licensing was done, but they never reached the scope of either the Disney Studios or Hanna-Barbera Productions in merchandising. Consequently, there just isn't as much stuff for a Warner Brothers collector. But there is an ample supply.

Certainly the 1990s introduction of The Warner Brothers Store to nearly every big city shopping mall will help cultivate continued interest in collecting Bugs Bunny memorabilia. Like Disney, there are increasing numbers of Warner Brothers collectors who have been introduced to limited edition sculptures, studio animation art, sericels (manufactured collectible cel art), and figures. With more and more of these new collectors stepping into the marketplace, the demand for vintage Warner Brothers character merchandise is bound to increase.

Collectors of vintage Warner Brothers characters don't have the national networking that exists for Disneyana collecting, but that may soon change with the increased activity on the Internet for collecting all cartoon characters. Collecting of early Bugs and the gang is due for an explosive move in the market place. This is one area of character collecting that has been too long overlooked and is currently vastly underrated. If I were the speculative collector, I'd be buying all the early Bugs toys I could afford right now.

As it stands today, Looney Tunes collectors have some wonderful Warner Brothers character toys to collect. What the Merrie Melodies friends lack in color (let's face it, Bugs, Daffy, Elmer, and Sylvester just aren't that visually stunning in regard to color palette), they make up for in humor and design. I'm a life-long Disneyana collector, but a Bugs Bunny cartoon is funnier to watch than most Mickey titles. Old Bugs Bunny was one funny guy, and collecting toys to remind us of that "silly wabbit" is a tangible way to keep in touch with that sly, sarcastic, elusive rabbit.

The Moss banks, the stunning figures by Shaw Pottery, the colorful books and puzzles from the golden years, and the rare pull toys by Brice Toys (not Fisher-Price) are all great reminders of a fun cast of characters that has always seemed to play second string to Mickey Mouse and friends.

But this is one rabbit whose story is not over. He has a new store line that's in every major city. He starred with Michael Jordan in *Space Jam* and stole the show. His vintage toys are currently a bargain in the toy collecting marketplace, but that may soon change as a new generation rediscovers Bugs. The slow old tortoise may have won in the fable, but this is one rabbit who is ready for a comeback. The ship for the Looney Tunes characters may be about to come in.

I'd bet my carrots on it!

Looney Tunes Merrie Melodies Comic Book by Dell Comics, ©Leon Schlesinger, early 1940s, $35.00 – 70.00.

Early Bugs Bunny Ceramic Figure by Evan K. Shaw Pottery, ©Warner Brothers, 1940s, $250.00 – 400.00.

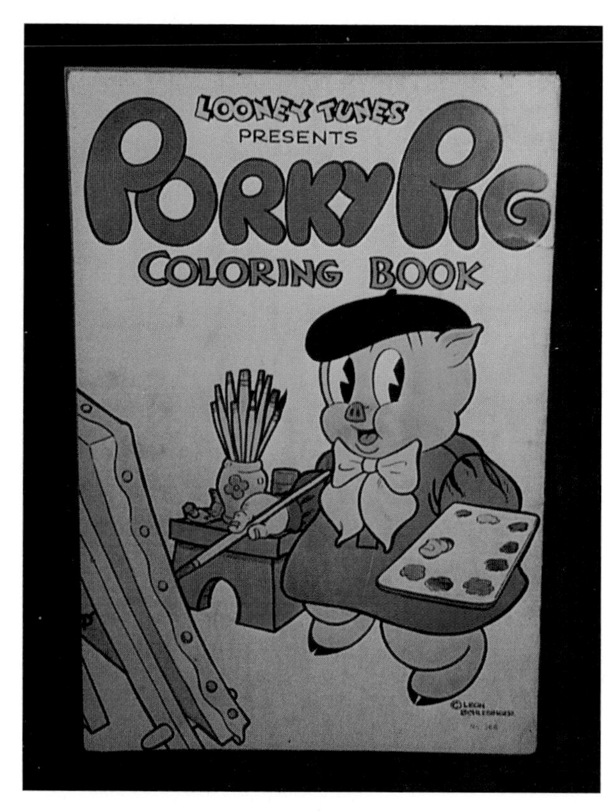

Looney Tunes presents Porky Pig Coloring Book, ©Leon Schlesinger, 1930s. Shows very early Porky Pig character on cover, $125.00 – 175.00.

Porky Pig's Duck Hunt, linen-like Story Book, ©Leon Schlesinger, 1930s. Rare, $145.00 – 200.00.

Elmer Fudd Fire Chief Wood Litho Pull Toy by Brice, ©Warner Brothers, 1940s. Features pull along bell ringing action. Brice Co. Toys are rare among cartoon designs, $175.00 – 250.00.

Cartoon-O-Craft Molding and Coloring Set, "Merrie Melodies," ©Warner Brothers Cartoons. Large craft casting set with molds of Bugs, Elmer, Daffy, etc., $95.00 – 140.00.

Porky the Bandmaster Ceramic Cup, ©Leon Schlesinger, 1940s, $75.00 – 100.00.

Sniffles Cast Iron Pot Metal Planter by Moss, ©Warner Bros., $125.00 – 200.00.

Bugs Bunny and Porky Pig Sip Mates Soda Straw Holders and Napkin Set, ©Leon Schlesinger, 1940s. Rare set, $150.00 – 225.00.

Sip Mates Straws and Novelties from boxed set pictured at left.

Elmer Fudd Bank by Moss, ©Warner Bros., $125.00 – 200.00.

Bugs Bunny Pot Metal Bank by Moss, ©Warner Brothers, $125.00 – 200.00.

Daffy Duck Planter by Moss, ©Warner Bros., $125.00 – 200.00.

Porky Pig Looney Tunes Bank by Moss, Warner Bros., 1940s, $125.00 – 200.00.

Beaky Bank by Moss, ©Warner Bros., $125.00 – 200.00.

Porky Pig Character Bank, metal, by Moss, ©Warner Brothers, $125.00 – 200.00.

Bugs Bunny Merrie Melodies Paint Book, ©Leon Schlesinger. Early Bugs paper example, $100.00 – 145.00.

Bugs Bunny Character Bank by Moss, ©Warner Brothers, $125.00 – 200.00.

Bugs Bunny as Davy Crockett, unusual garb for this Warner Bros. character but all original and all fun, $350.00 – 500.00.

Elmer Fudd Child's Mask, ©Warner Bros., $60.00 – 90.00.

Porky Pig Rubber Squeak Toy by Sun Rubber, ©Warner Brothers, $50.00 – 75.00.

Very early Porky Pig Figural Bank, ©Warner Brothers, circa 1930s. Bisque painted figural construction, $150.00 – 200.00.

Sniffles Mouse Figure by Evan K. Shaw, ©Warner Bros., $135.00 – 210.00.

Warner Brothers Ceramic Decanters, $50.00 – 75.00.

Small Sniffles "Shaw" Figure, ©W.B., $75.00 – 125.00.

Bugs Bunny Shaw Figures, ©Warner Brothers, $150.00 – 200.00.

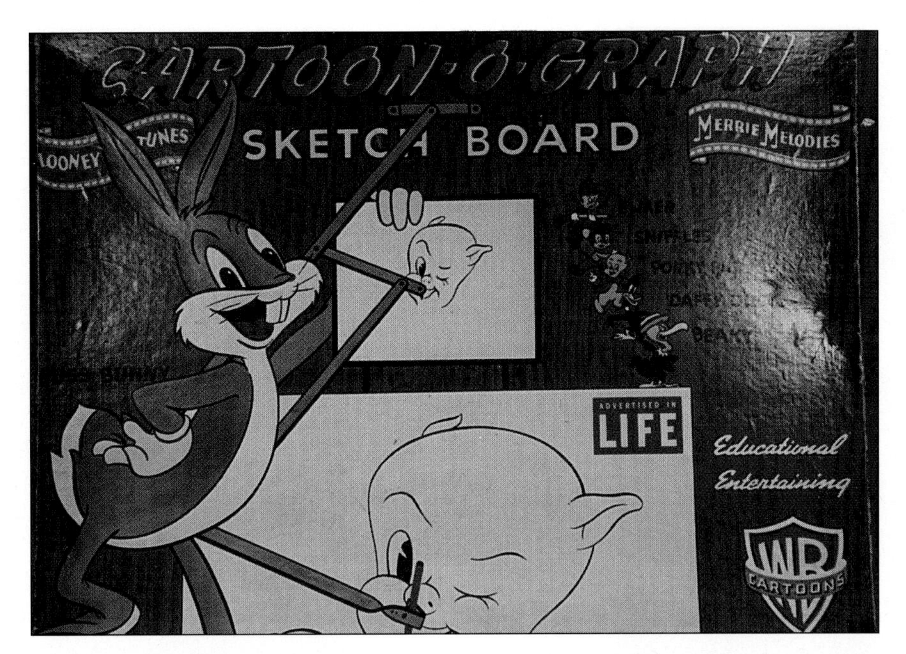

Cartoon-O-Graph Sketch Board "Merrie Melodies" ©Warner Brothers, 1950s.
Used for copying "sketches" of Warner Brothers characters, $125.00 – 175.00.

Inside view of Cartoon-O-Graph Sketch Board.

Bugs Bunny cloth and plastic-faced large Doll, ©Warner Brothers, 1950s, $75.00 – 125.00.

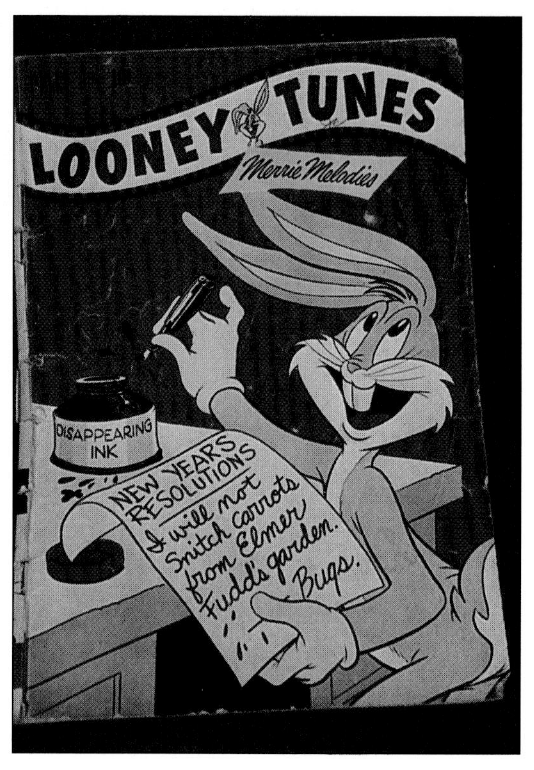

Looney Tunes Bugs Bunny Movie Melodies Comic Book by Dell Comics, ©Warner Brothers, 1950s, $25.00 – 40.00.

"I taut I taw a Puddy-Tat" Warner Bros. Sheet Music, pub. by Remick Music Corp., $15.00 – 25.00.

Tweety Pie Soft Rubber Squeak Toy, probably 1930s. Rubber is very pliable and these are often found in poor condition, $75.00 – 125.00.

Bugs Bunny Vase by Shaw Pottery, ©Warner Brothers, $175.00 – 350.00.

Bugs Bunny Ceramic Figure, manufactured by Evan K. Shaw Pottery, ©Warner Brothers, $150.00 – 300.00.

Daffy Duck Ceramic Figure by Evan K. Shaw Pottery, ©Warner Bros., $150.00 – 300.00.

Elmer Fudd Bud Vase by Shaw, ©Warner Bros., $150.00 – 275.00.

Bugs Bunny Soft Rubber Squeak Toy, gray version, 1930s, $150.00 – 200.00.

Bugs Bunny Soft Rubber Squeak Toy, beige version, 1930s, $135.00 – 175.00.

Bugs Bunny with Cart Ceramic Planter, ©Warner Brothers, $75.00. – 100.00.

Sniffles the Mouse Ceramic Figure by Evan K. Shaw Pottery, ©Warner Brothers, 1940s, $125.00 – 200.00.

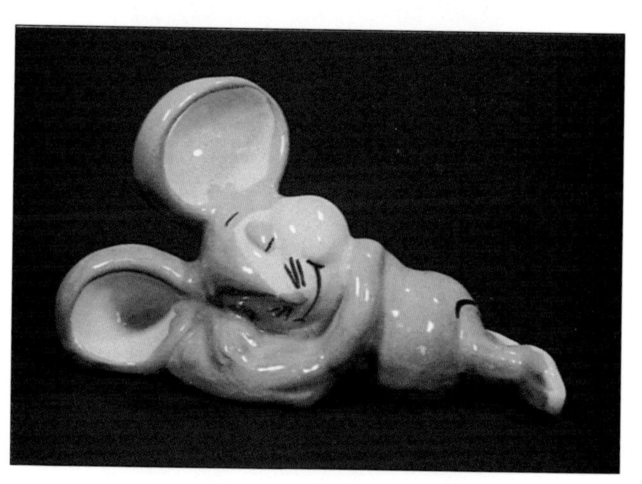

Sleeping Sniffles the Mouse by Evan K. Shaw Pottery, ©Warner Brothers, $75.00 – 135.00.

Bugs Bunny Ceramic Figure by Evan K. Shaw Pottery, $100.00 – 175.00.

Porky Pig Glazed Ceramic Figure by Evan K. Shaw, ©Warner Brothers, 1940s, $125.00 – 200.00.

Petunia Pig Glazed Ceramic Figure by Evan K. Shaw, ©Warner Brothers, 1940s, $125.00 – 200.00.

Bugs Bunny Ceramic Planter, ©Warner Brothers, circa 1940s, $65.00 – 95.00.

Bugs Bunny Frame Tray Puzzle by Whitman, ©Warner Brothers, $35.00 – 50.00.

Bugs Bunny and Aladdin's Lamp Children's Record by Capitol Records, ©Warner Brothers. With extremely colorful record jacket, $50.00 – 75.00.

Bugs Bunny and the Tortoise, Warner Brothers version of The Tortoise and the Hare Story, with picture book inside, ©Warner Bros., 45 rpm set, $25.00 – 50.00.

Bugs Bunny meets Hiawatha Child's Record, by Capitol Records, ©Warner Brothers, $25.00 – 40.00.

Bugs Bunny and Elmer Fudd Inlaid Frame Tray Puzzle, ©Warner Brothers, 1950s, $40.00 – 60.00.

Bugs Bunny Baseball Player Doll holding cloth carrot with pressed cloth face, ©Warner Brothers. Rare, $250.00 – 400.00.

Bugs Bunny – Porky Pig Paint Book by Leon Schlesinger, 1940s, $75.00 – 125.00.

Bugs Bunny Tricycle Pull Toy by Brice Toys, ©Warner Brothers, circa 1940, . One of the very few Bugs pull toy designs ever made, $400.00 – 600.00.

Porky Pig in Desert Adventure by Dell Comics, ©Warner Bros. and Leon Schlesinger, $30.00 – 60.00.

Tweety's Puddy Tat Twouble Record and Book by Capitol Records, ©Warner Brothers, $75.00 – 100.00.

Detail of inside of Picture Book Record.

Warner Bros. 1977 Christmas Plate, ©Warner Bros., $25.00 – 50.00.

Looney Tunes Merrie Melodies Paint Book, ©Leon Schlesinger, 1940s, $65.00 – 95.00.

Porky Pig Composition Bank, 1930s. Rare, $225.00 – 375.00.

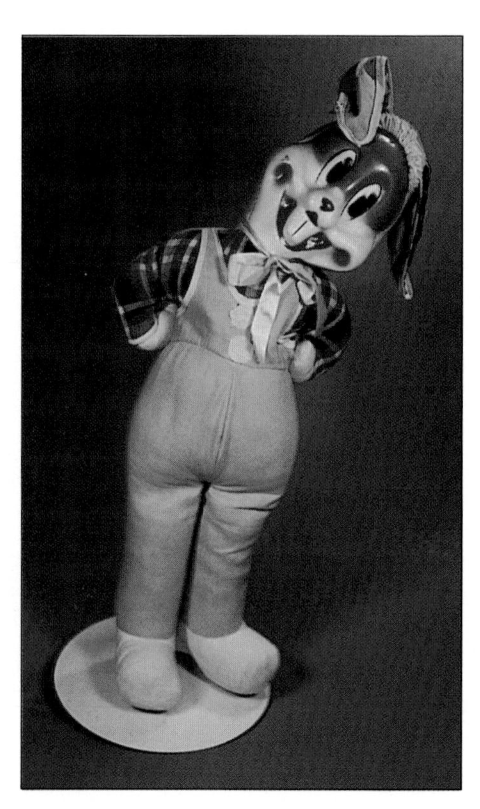

Bugs Bunny Cloth and Vinyl Character Doll, ©Warner Brothers, 1950s, $60.00 – 85.00.

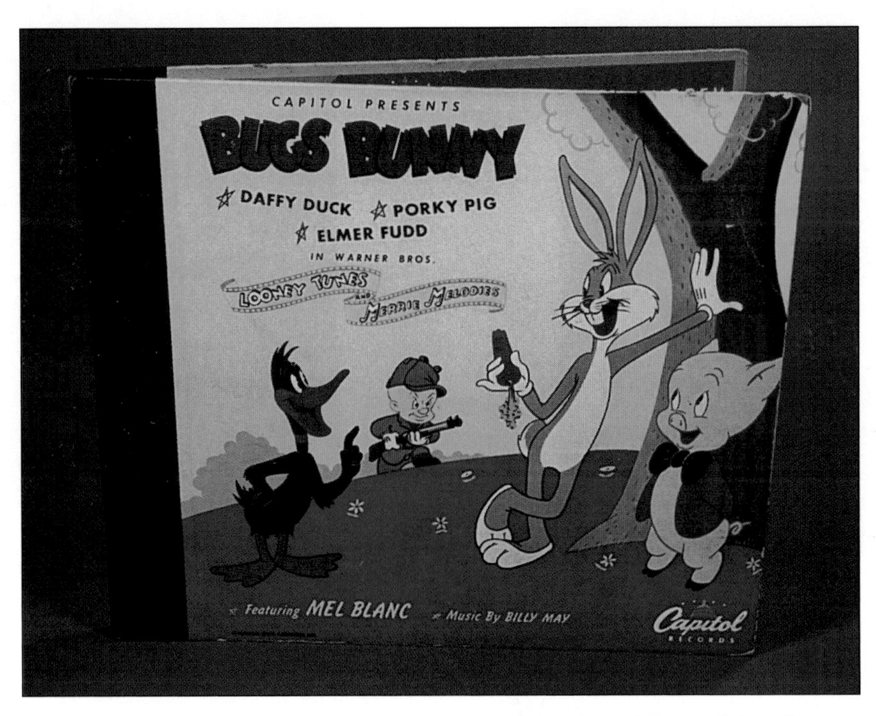

"Capitol presents Bugs Bunny," 78rpm Storybook and Record Set, featuring Mel Blanc, ©Warner Bros. $75.00 – 100.00.

Detail of Bugs Bunny illustration inside Storybook of Record Set above.

Additional detail of Storybook pages in Record Set above showing great illustration of Elmer Fudd as a Farmer.

Porky Pig Framed Nursery Print, ©Warner Brothers Cartoons, Inc., circa 1950, $35.00 – 55.00.

Bugs Bunny in Risky Business, Big Little Books, ©Warner Brothers, $40.00 – 65.00.

"Tweety Pie" Squeak Toy, unusual, very soft rubber, ©Warner Brothers, 1940s, $75.00 – 125.00.

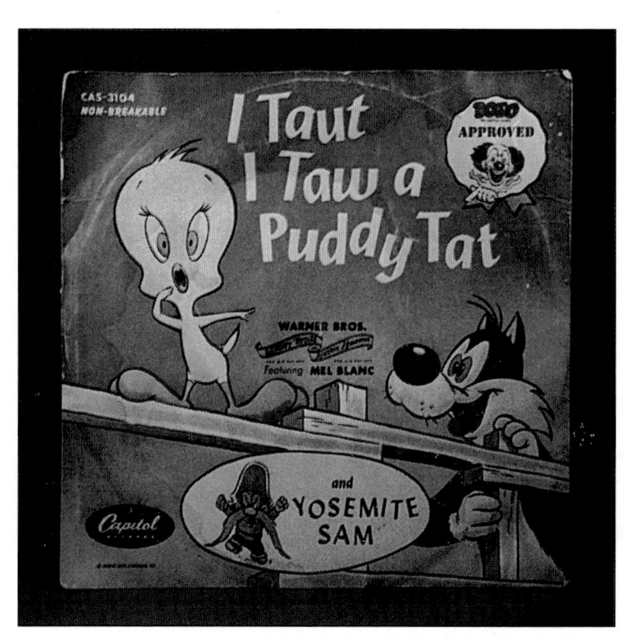

Tweetie and Sylvester Record by Capitol Records, 78rpm, ©Warner Brothers 1950s, $25.00 – 50.00.

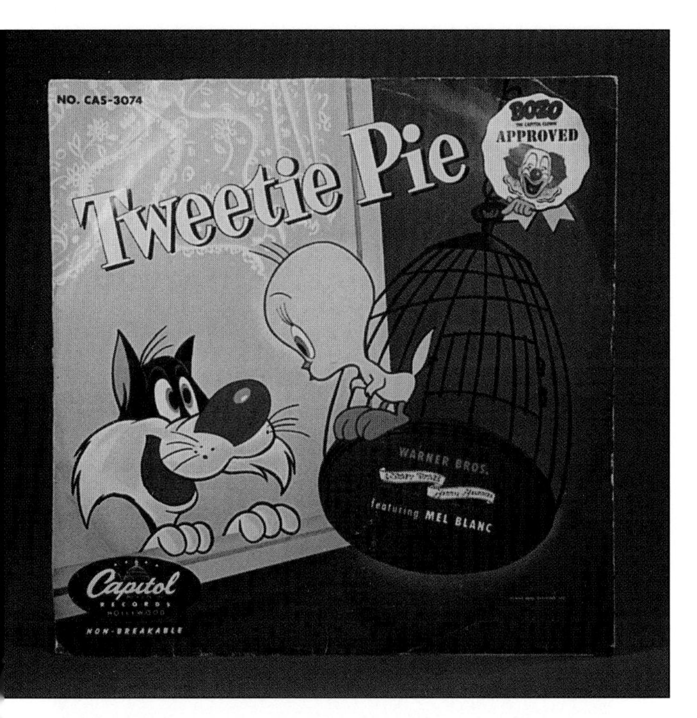

Tweetie Pie Capitol Record for Children, 78rpm, ©Warner Brothers, $25.00 – 50.00.

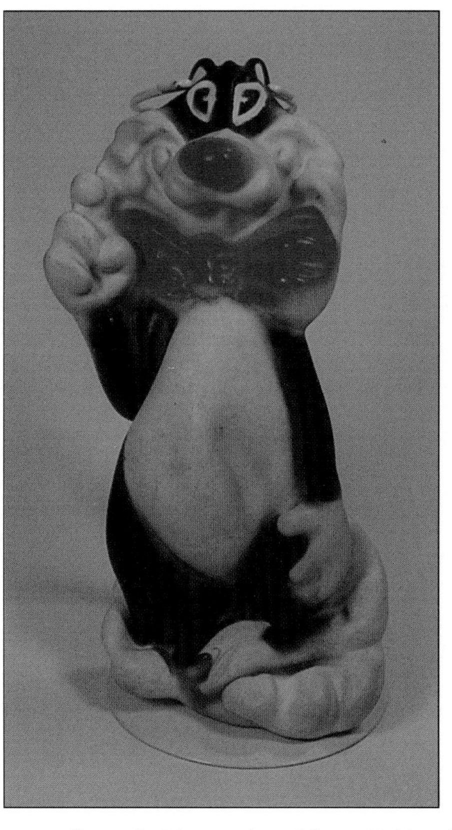

Rare Sylvester Squeak Toy, soft rubber, 1930s, $125.00 – 175.00.

Bugs Bunny Better Little Book, ©Warner Bros., 1940s, $25.00 – 40.00.

Bugs Bunny's Mistake, Tiny Book ©Warner Bros., $12.00 – 25.00. Bugs Charity Button, ©Warner Bros., $10.00 – 15.00.

Bugs Bunny Character Ceramic Bud Vase, ©Warner Brothers, $75.00 – 100.00.

Bugs Bunny Print for framing, ©Warner Brothers Cartoons, $50.00 – 75.00.

Porky Pig Print for framing, ©Warner Brothers Cartoons, $50.00 – 75.00.

Bugs Bunny Ceramic Planter, ©Warner Brothers, circa 1940s, $85.00 – 125.00.

Bugs Bunny 78rpm Album with Storybook inside, Capitol Records, ©Warner Brothers, $50.00 – 75.00.

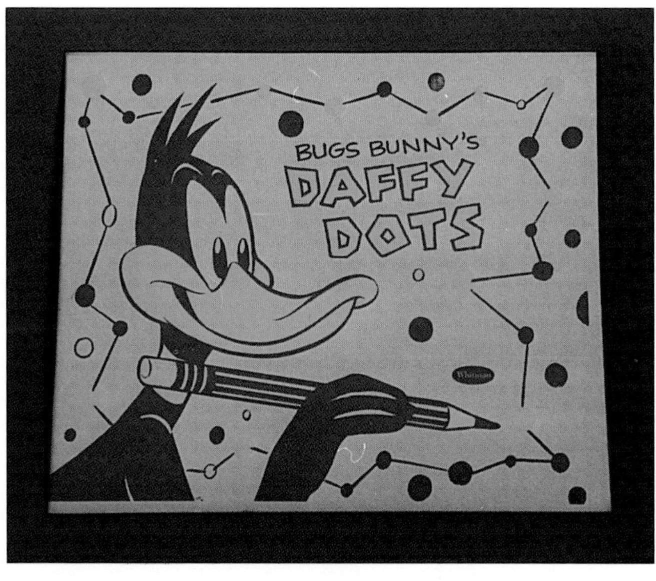

Bugs Bunny's Daffy Dots Book by Whitman, ©Warner Brothers, $15.00 – 30.00.

Bugs Bunny March of Comics Premium Comic give-away, $25.00 – 40.00.

Bugs Bunny Coloring Book by Whitman, ©Warner Brothers. Unusual Graphics on cover with Bugs' Indian Chief hat made of crayons instead of feathers, $35.00 – 50.00.

Bugs Bunny Baker Man Children's Storybook, ©Warner Brothers Cartoons, Inc., $25.00 – 45.00.

Bugs Bunny Soaky Character Toy, ©Warner Brothers, $20.00 – 30.00.

Bugs Bunny boxed 45rpm Record Set, Capitol Records, ©Warner Brothers, $25.00 – 50.00.

Bugs Bunny Talking Alarm Clock by Equity, ©Warner Brothers. Battery operated, $125.00 – 200.00.

Sylvester and Hippety Hopper Child's Story Record, ©Warner Bros. on Capitol Records with Bozo logo, $20.00 – 35.00.

Warner Brothers Characters Whiskey Decanters, from recent series of all Warner Brothers Figures, ©Warner Brothers, $50.00 – 75.00 each.

Bugs Bunny's Magic Rub-off Pictures "with Kleenex Tissues for cleaning pictures," manufactured by Whitman, ©Warner Brothers, $75.00 – 100.00.

Small Elmer Fudd Shaw Figure, ©Warner Bros., $75.00 – 140.00.

Warner Brothers Character Thermos, ©Warner Bros., $60.00 – 85.00.

Bugs Tin Litho Figure, ©Warner Bros., 1950s, $75.00 – 100.00.

Bugs Bunny and Pals Cold Cups Box, assorted, $125.00 – 160.00.

Porky Pig and His Gang Big Little Book, 1930s, $35.00 – 70.00.

Looney Tunes Paint Book, ©Leon Schlesinger, late 1930s, $95.00 – 140.00.

Porky Pig Comics, "All Pictures," Schlesinger, 1930s, $40.00 – 65.00.

Warner Brothers Character Whiskey Decanters. From a recent set, $50.00 – 75.00 each.

Bugs Bunny Colorforms Cartoon Kit, early Colorforms set, ©Warner Brothers, $75.00 – 100.00.

Warner Brothers Character Plates, 1950s, $12.00 – 20.00 each.

Warner Brothers Character Plates, 1950s, $12.00 – 20.00 each.

Bugs Bunny and Pals Cups Set, ©Warner Bros., 1950s, $125.00 – 200.00.

Bugs Bunny Boxed Puppet Set by Zany Puppets with original Comic Book Script, 1950s. Although often sold as Bugs, this may be a non-authorized Bugs knock-off piece. (Note Rabbit on "comic" is not Bugs.) $50.00 – 75.00.

Bugs Bunny Character Doll, plastic face with satin type clothes, $110.00 – 175.00.

Bugs Bunny Soft Rubber Squeak Toy, ©Warner Bros., 1940 – 1950s, $75.00 – 100.00.

Looney Toons Character Lunch Box with television design, ©Warner Brothers, circa 1960s, $75.00 – 125.00.

Looney Toons Character Lunch Box, reverse side.

Looney Toons Character Lunch Box, side view.

Bugs Bunny and The Tortoise 78rpm Record Set and Storybook by Capitol Records, ©Warner Brothers, $35.00 – 60.00.

Large Bugs Bunny Plaster Composition Bank, ©Warner Brothers, circa 1950s, $150.00 – 275.00.

Bugs Bunny and Elmer Fudd Battery-operated Radio, ©Warner Brothers, recent, $45.00 – 70.00.

Porky Pig March of Comics Premium Book, ©Warner Brothers, $25.00 – 40.00.

Porky Pig Windup Cowboy, with original box, manufactured by Louis Marx, ©Warner Brothers, $600.00 – 850.00.

Tweety Coloring Book by Whitman, ©Warner Brothers, $25.00 – 45.00.

Porky Pig Plaster Lamp, ©Warner Brothers, $150.00 – 225.00.

Bugs Bunny Inlaid Puzzle, ©Warner Brothers, 1950s, $50.00 – 75.00.

Bugs Bunny Behind Tree Large Chalk Statue, probably 1940s. Great likeness of Bugs, $100.00 – 175.00.

Bugs Bunny Inlaid Puzzle, ©Warner Brothers, 1950s, $50.00 – 75.00.

Bugs Bunny Toot-A-Tune, with original box, ©Warner Brothers. Plastic flute actually plays notes, $100 – 150.00.

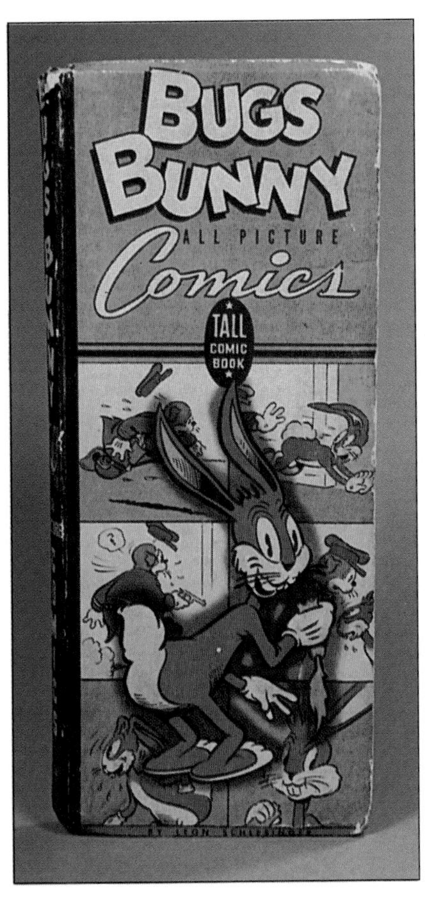

Bugs Bunny All Picture Comics, "Tall Comic Book" featuring a very early Bugs on cover, Leon Schlesinger, 1930s, $75.00 – 110.00.

Foghorn Leghorn Chicken Stuffed Animal, ©Warner Brothers, recent, $20.00 – 30.00.

Bugs Wall Picture, early, ©Leon Schlesinger. Part of a set of all the Schlesinger characters of the time, $50.00 – 75.00.

Foghorn Leghorn Character Puppet, ©Warner Brothers, 1970s, $20.00 – 30.00.

Foghorn Leghorn Character Glasses, ©Warner Brothers, $7.00 – 15.00 each.

Foghorn Leghorn New York Tray, ©Warner Brothers, recent, $20.00 – 30.00.

Foghorn Leghorn Warner Brothers Character Glasses, ©Warner Brothers, $7.00 – 15.00 each.

Foghorn Leghorn Stuffed Plush Toy, ©Warner Brothers, recent, $12.00 – 18.00.

DISNEY FEATURE CARTOON COLLECTIBLES

In the years leading up to 1937, Walt Disney and his animation artists at the studio knew they were on to something. Walt and his staff of animators had paid their dues for almost a decade in the short cartoon trade, building upon their basic skills and taking industry leading chances.

The Silly Symphonies series, introduced in the mid 1930s, allowed the Walt Disney Studios to perfect color animation, special effects, superior background art, characterization, and story development. The use of the 3-D multi-plane camera allowed animated shots to have a true depth of field never before seen. It was inevitable that successes in all these areas would lead Walt Disney to the challenge of creating the first full-length animated feature.

Most people in the industry scoffed at the presumption by Disney that adults and children alike would sit still for a one-hour-plus cartoon. It just hadn't been done. Cartoons were good, but nobody wanted to go to the movies to see just a cartoon! They were just for intermission.

Walt changed all that. With the studio's premiere of *Snow White and The Seven Dwarfs* in 1937, Disney proved to the world that cartoon characters could be actors and that they could sustain an audience's interest for the length of a feature.

Thus, the film characters of Disney's feature films became immediate prime subjects for marketing and merchandising. The toys pictured in this chapter are a sample of those available from Disney's "golden years" – the years when the studio was breaking new ground with one animated film hit after another. From *The Three Little Pigs* (actually a long silly symphony) to *Snow White, Ferdinand, Pinocchio, Bambi, Lady and The Tramp, Cinderella,* and others, this chapter takes the reader through a colorful sampling of only a small amount of the hundreds of toys marketed with the release of every new Disney cartoon feature since *Snow White.*

Certainly the great new Disney film releases of the 1980s and 1990s, including *The Little Mermaid, Beauty and The Beast, The Lion King,* and *Aladdin,* will make their own marks on the collecting world of the future. The older release toys are pictured here because they are a little harder to find, but toys from the recent releases, once out of original production, are also increasing in value.

This chapter is intended to be a return to old friends for advanced Disney collectors and an introduction to some golden age Disney collectibles for those who are new fans of vintage Disney features.

This author's favorite Disney song of all time is the tune Jiminy Cricket crooned that evening long ago in Geppetto's bedroom, "When You Wish Upon a Star."

With Pinocchio, Snow White, and all their friends, may these toy characters from some of Walt Disney's best works touch that special place inside you.

May they all help each novice or advanced collector to leaf through the pages and once again "wish" upon that wishing star....

Ingersoll Three Little Pigs Pocket Watch in original box, W. Disney Enterprises, 1930s, $1,500.00 – 2,000.00.

Walt Disney's Own Game Red Riding Hood, manufactured by Parker Brothers, ©Walt Disney Ent. 1930s, $150.00 – 225.00.

Exterior of Three Little Pigs Watch box. Note original purchase price was $1.50.

Three Little Pigs Glazed Ceramic Three Pigs Toothbrush Holder, knock-off unauthorized version, $75.00 – 125.00.

Three Little Pigs Sand Pail by Ohio Art, ©Walt Disney Ent., $150.00 – 300.00.

Three Little Pigs Wood-backed Jigsaw Puzzle, French, ©Walt Disney, 1930s, $125.00 – 200.00.

Who's Afraid of the Big Bad Wolf Three Little Pigs Bisque Set, Japan, ©Walt Disney, distributed by George Borgfeldt Co., $400.00 – 700.00.

Three Little Pigs Sprinkling Can by Ohio Art Co. of Bryan, Ohio, ©Walt Disney Ent., 1930s, $125.00 – 200.00.

Three Little Pigs Wash Tub by Ohio Art, ©Walt Disney Enterprises, 1930s, $125.00 – 200.00.

Three Little Pigs Tiny 3" Pail by Ohio Art, ©Walt Disney Ent., 1930s, $75.00 – 150.00.

Three Little Pigs Lusterware Ashtray, ©W. Disney, 1930s, $75.00 – 135.00.

Three Little Pigs Divided Dish by Patriot China, ©Walt Disney Ent., 1930s, $150.00 – 225.00.

Elmer Elephant Child's China Plate, Japan, ©Walt Disney, 1930s, $75.00 – 100.00.

Three Little Pigs Boxed Lusterware Tea Set, ©Walt Disney Enterprises. Rarest of all Disney character china sets, $400.00 – 650.00.

"Walt Disney's Ferdinand the Bull" Doll, wood composition by Ideal Toy and Novelty with original box, 1930s, $250.00 – 400.00.

Ferdinand's Chinese Checkers with The Bee Marble Game by Parker Brothers, 1930s, $125.00 – 175.00.

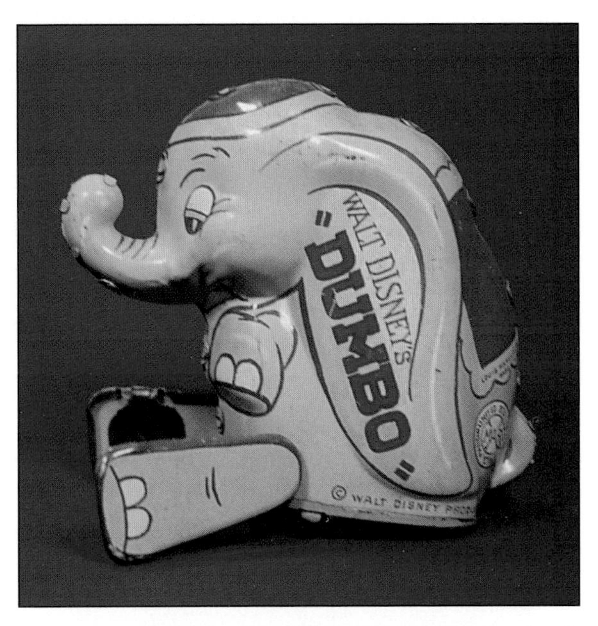

Walt Disney's Dumbo Tumbling Wind-up Toy by Louis Marx, ©Walt Disney Prod., $350.00 – 550.00.

Ferdinand the Bull Tin Wind-up Toy by Marx, Walt Disney Ent., 1938, $800.00 – 1,000.00.

Ferdinand the Bull Chalk Figure, with flower in mouth and unusual green paint, 1930s, $95.00 – 140.00.

Walt Disney's Snow White and The Seven Dwarfs Paint Book, large format, ©Walt Disney Enterprises, 1938, $75.00 – 125.00.

Ferdinand the Bull Composition Bank by Crown Toy and Novelty, Walt Disney Enterprises, 1938, $125.00 – 200.00.

Snow White and The Seven Dwarfs Celluloid Baby Rattle, with colorful characters all the way around the sides, ©Walt Disney Ent., 1930s, $150.00 – 225.00.

Snow White Cloth Faced Doll in original dress, manufactured by Ideal Toy and Novelty, ©Walt Disney Enterprises, 1930s, $325.00 – 500.00.

Happy the Dwarf Doll by Richard Krueger of New York, ©Walt Disney, circa 1930s, $275.00 – 450.00.

Dopey Dwarf Doll by Alexander Doll, in original box, 1930s, $375.00 – 550.00.

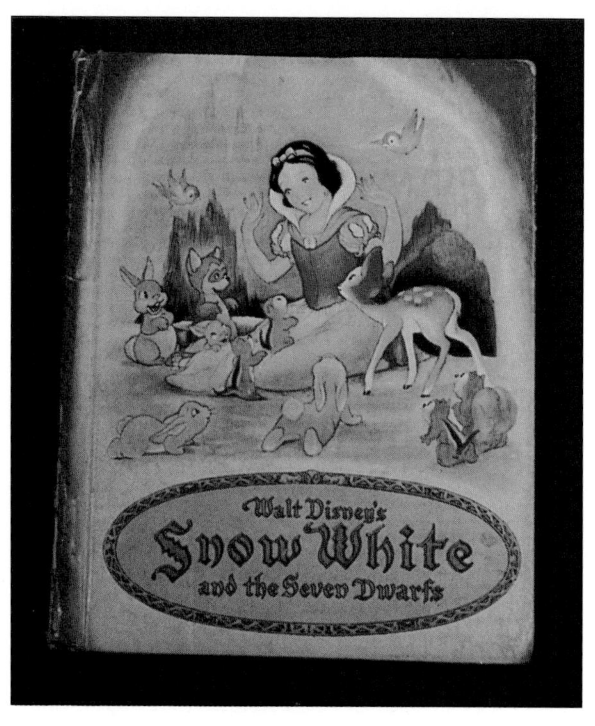

Walt Disney's Snow White and The Seven Dwarfs Small Picture Storybook, 1938, $50.00 – 75.00.

Walt Disney's Snow White and The Seven Dwarfs Linen-like Book, authorized edition, Walt Disney Enterprises, 1938, $75.00 – 125.00.

Inside illustration page of Snow White Book.

Back cover of Book in above photo.

Walt Disney's Snow White and The Seven Dwarfs Picture Puzzle Set, with two pictures in the box, Walt Disney Ent., 1938, $125.00 – 200.00.

Snow White Tin Litho Container, Belgian or French manufacturer, ©Walt Disney, 1930s, $225.00 – 375.00.

Dopey Night Light, manufactured by Nite Lite, Co., circa 1930s and copyright Walt Disney Enterprises, $300.00 – 500.00.

Walt Disney's Snow White Radio by Emerson Electric featuring wood composition "sculptured" character panels on front, circa 1938, $1,200.00 – 1,700.00.

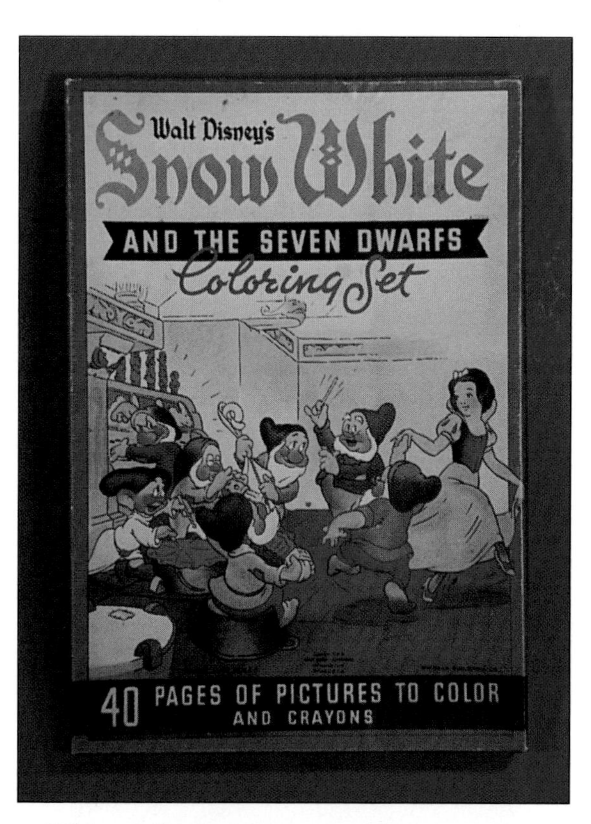

Snow White Coloring Set containing crayons and 40 coloring sheets, manufactured by Whitman, Walt Disney Ent., 1938, $150.00 – 225.00.

Dopey Marx Wind-up Walker Toy, ©Walt Disney Enterprises, 1938, $425.00 – 600.00.

Large Happy the Dwarf Doll, 1930s, probably by Knickerbocker, ©Walt Disney Enterprises, $300.00 – 475.00.

Dopey Dwarf Doll by Chad Valley of England, 1930s, $250.00 – 400.00.

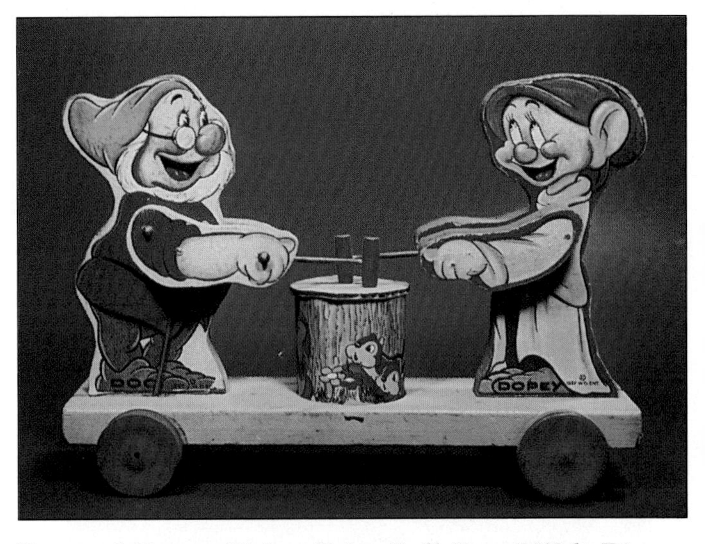

Doc and Dopey Fisher-Price Pull Toy, ©Walt Disney Enterprises, 1938, $400.00 – 750.00.

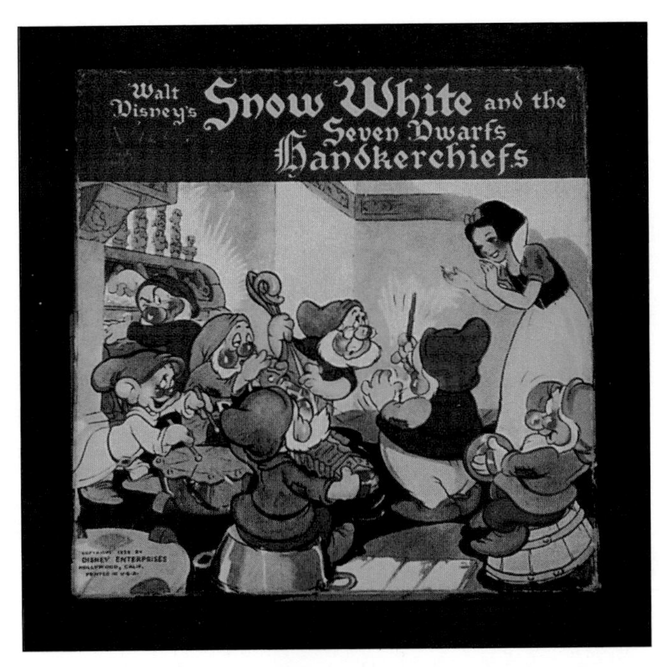

Snow White and The Seven Dwarfs Handkerchiefs, boxed set, 1938, $150.00 – 225.00.

Dopey Bank, wood composition by Crown Toy and Novelty, ©Walt Disney Ent., 1938, $250.00 – 400.00.

Snow White 5" Tin Sand Pail by Ohio Art, ©Walt Disney Ent., 1938, $250.00 – 400.00.

Walt Disney's Snow White and The Seven Dwarfs Paint Book, Whitman, Walt Disney Enterprises, 1937, $60.00 – 95.00.

Seven Dwarfs Set of Hard Rubber Figures by Seiberling Latex Products of Akron, Ohio, ©Walt Disney Enterprises. Value is for set of seven, $300.00 – 550.00.

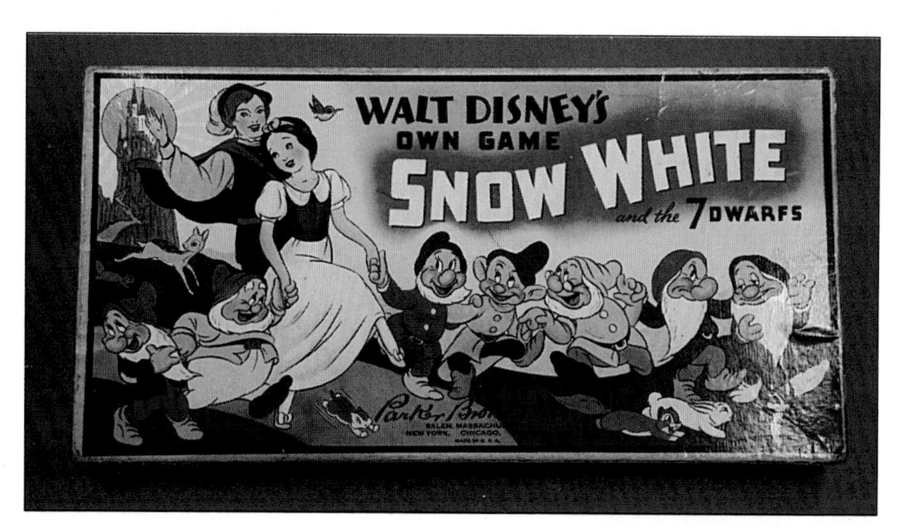

Walt Disney's Snow White Game by Parker Brothers, ©Walt Disney Ent., 1938, $200.00 – 300.00.

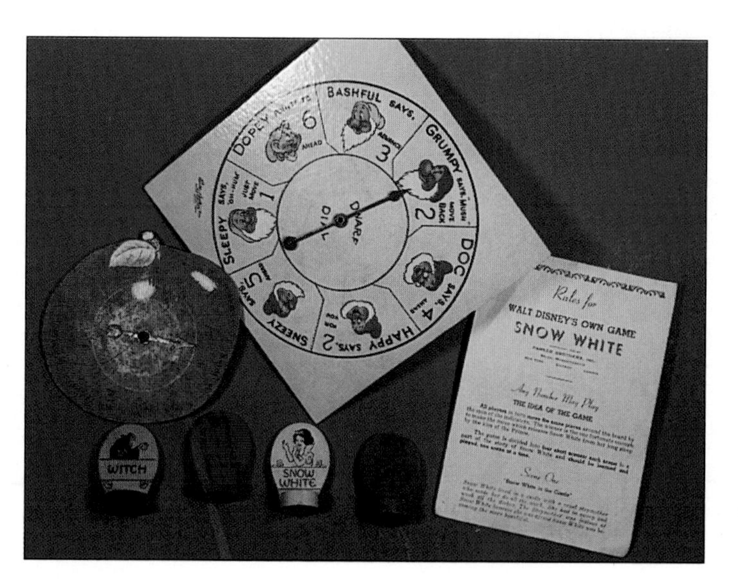

Inside game pieces for Snow White Game pictured above.

Snow White Composition Character Doll by Knickerbocker, ©Walt Disney Enterprises, 1938, $375.00 – 550.00.

Sneezy Composition Doll by Knickerbocker, with original wrist tag, 1938, $325.00 – 500.00.

Dopey Composition Character Doll by Knickerbocker, ©Walt Disney Enterprises, 1938, $325.00 – 500.00.

Bashful Composition Dwarf Doll by Knickerbocker, Walt Disney Enterprises, 1938, $325.00 – 500.00.

Happy the Dwarf Doll by Knickerbocker, with original wrist tag, ©W.D. Ent., 1938, $325.00 – 500.00.

Doc the Dwarf Doll by Knickerbocker, ©Walt Disney Ent. with original wrist tag, wool beard, composition body, velvet clothes, 1938, $325.00 – 500.00.

Sleepy the Dwarf Doll by Knickerbocker with original factory wrist tag, Walt Disney Enterprises, 1938, $325.00 – 500.00.

Grumpy the Dwarf Character Doll by Knickerbocker, ©Walt Disney Enterprises, 1938, $325.00 – 500.00.

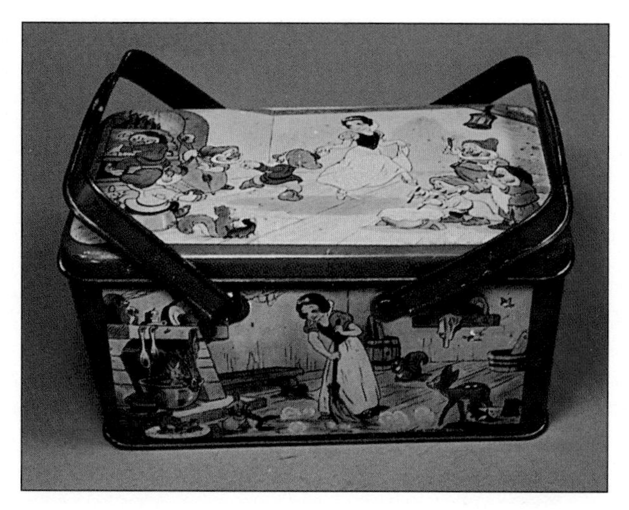

Snow White Tin Litho Lunch Box, showing colorful scenes from the original Disney film, European manufacture, ©Walt Disney, 1938, $300.00 – 400.00.

Top view of Snow White Lunch Tin.

Side view of Snow White Lunch Tin.

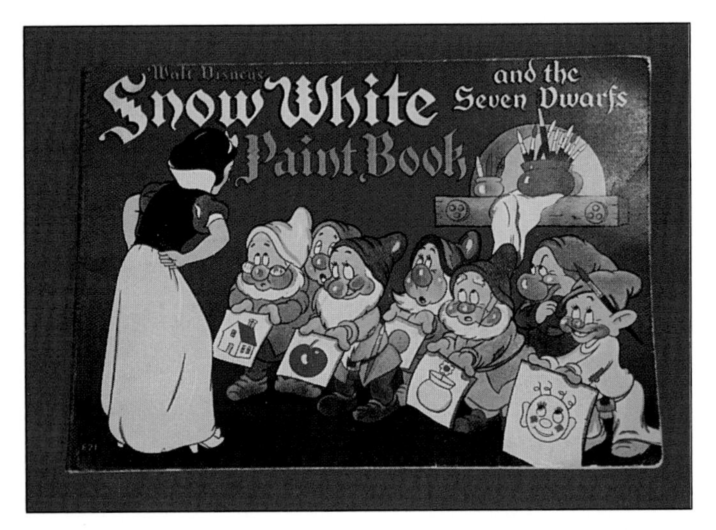

Snow White and The Seven Dwarfs Paint Book, published by Whitman, Walt Disney Enterprises, 1938, $75.00 – 100.00.

Snow White Movie Lobby Card, 11" x 14", ©Walt Disney, circa 1940s, $65.00 – 90.00.

Snow White Movie Lobby Card, Walt Disney Studios, 1940s, $65.00 – 90.00.

Walt Disney's Snow White and The Seven Dwarfs Scrap Book, Walt Disney Ent., 1938, $125.00 – 200.00.

Snow White Big Little Book, ©W.D. Ent., 1938, $50.00 – 75.00.

Walt Disney's Paint Book, animals from Snow White, Walt Disney Enterprises, 1938, $75.00 – 125.00.

Snow White Composition Doll by Knickerbocker in original box with original wrist tag, 1938, $750.00 – 1,000.00.

Snow White Pull Toy by N.N. Hill Brass, ©W.D. Ent., 1938, $500.00 – 700.00.

Dopey Composition Plaster Lamp by La Mode Studios, W.D. Ent., 1938, $500.00 – 750.00.

Snow White and Sneezy Character Glasses, with unusual color decal labels, ©W.D. Ent., 1937, $60.00 – 90.00.

Snow White Glass Ornaments, ©W.D. Ent., 1938, $750.00 – 900.00.

Snow White Ornaments box, opened.

Bashful and Happy Snow White Character Glasses, ©Walt Disney, 1937, $60.00 – 90.00 each.

Doc and Grumpy Disney Dwarf Character Glasses, unusual color decal on glasses, ©Walt Disney, 1937, $60.00. – 90.00.

Sleepy and Dopey Disney Dwarf Character Glasses, ©Walt Disney, circa 1937, $60.00 – 90.00 each.

Snow White English Ceramic Toothpick Holder by S. Maw and Sons, 1938, $300.00 – 450.00.

Snow White Valentines, ©W.D. Ent., 1938, $30.00 – 60.00.

Doc the Dwarf English Toothpick Holder, by S. Maw and Sons, 1938, $275.00 – 400.00.

Snow White Boxed Puzzles, 1938, ©W.D. Enterprises by Whitman, $125.00 – 200.00.

Snow White Celluloid Baby Rattle, ©Walt Disney Enterprises, circa 1938, $150.00 – 250.00.

Joe Carioca the Parrot Disney Character, manufactured by American Pottery, ©Walt Disney Production, circa 1940s, $125.00 – 200.00.

Dopey the Drummer Pull Toy, manufactured by Fisher-Price Toys, copyright Walt Disney Enterprises, 1938, $300.00 – 500.00.

Pinocchio Delivery Wind-up Pull Back Action Tin Delivery Cart by Marx, Walt Disney Productions, 1940. Rare Disney toy example, $950.00 – 1,400.00.

Pinocchio Fisher-Price Pull Toy, ©Walt Disney. Very rare Fisher-Price example, circa 1939, $600.00 – 950.00.

Pinocchio Doll by Ideal Toy and Novelty, 1940. Doll features arms and legs that are multi-jointed to give the figure many posing possibilities, along with original felt hat and attached cloth bow tie. Shown with original box, $600.00 – 850.00.

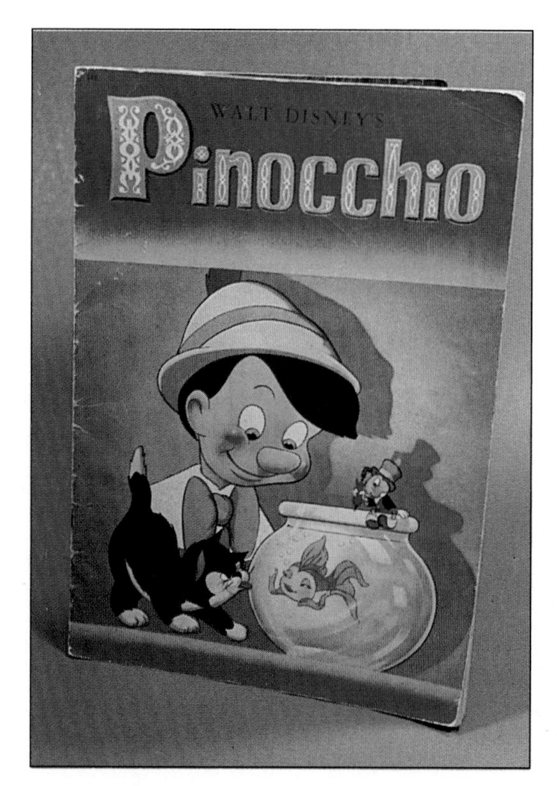

Walt Disney's Pinocchio Picture Book, Walt Disney, 1939. Featuring full color pictures throughout, $75.00 – 100.00.

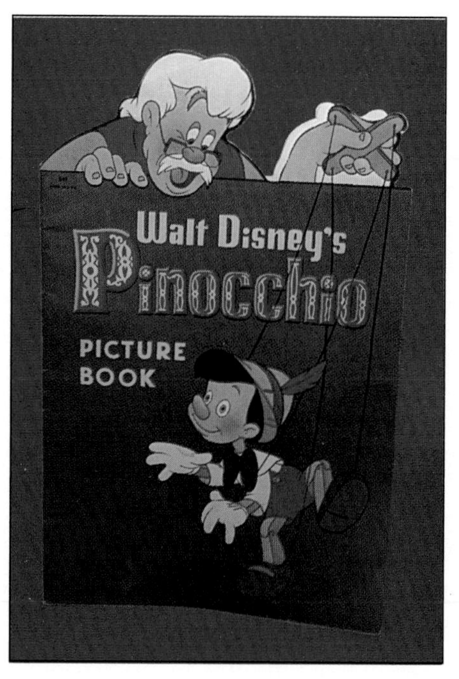

Walt Disney's Pinocchio Picture Book, ©Walt Disney Enterprises, 1939. Note unusual die-cut edge on top of book and all inside pages, $95.00 – 145.00.

Walt Disney's Pinocchio School Tablet, Walt Disney Productions, 1939, $75.00 – 125.00.

Pinocchio Composition Figure with movable arms by Crown Toy and Novelty, ©Walt Disney Enterprises, 1939, $125.00 – 200.00.

Pinocchio Doll by Knickerbocker Toy, shown wearing original clothes, ©Walt Disney Enterprises, 1939, $450.00 – 700.00.

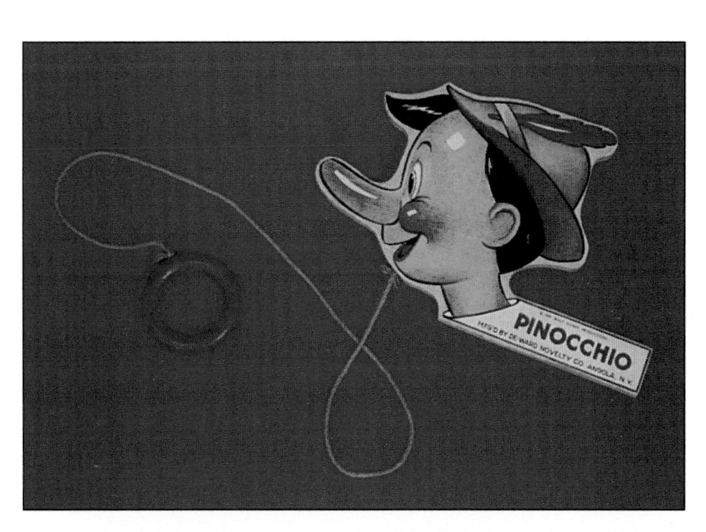

Pinocchio Ring Toss Game, ©W.D. Prod., 1939, $75.00 – 125.00.

Pinocchio and Jiminy Cricket Wind-up Toys by Line Mar of Japan, $400.00 – 650.00.

Walt Disney's Pinocchio Color Box, marked Walt Disney Prod., 1940s. Contains watercolor paints, $50.00 – 100.00.

Pinocchio Puzzle by Whitman, Walt Disney Productions, 1939, $50.00 – 75.00 single puzzle value.

The largest of all known Pinocchio Dolls! This one is 30" tall and "life sized," manufactured by Knickerbocker Toys, ©Walt Disney, 1939, $1,800.00 – 3,000.00.

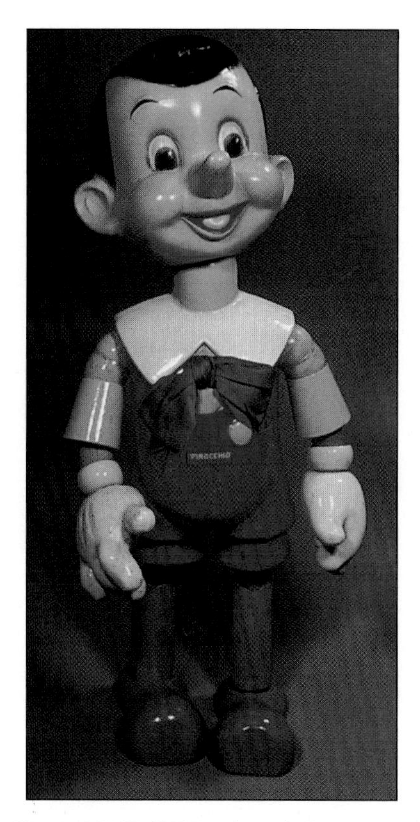

Pinocchio Giant 20" Tall Wood and Composition Doll by Ideal Toy and Novelty, Walt Disney Prod., 1939, $750.00 – 1,000.00.

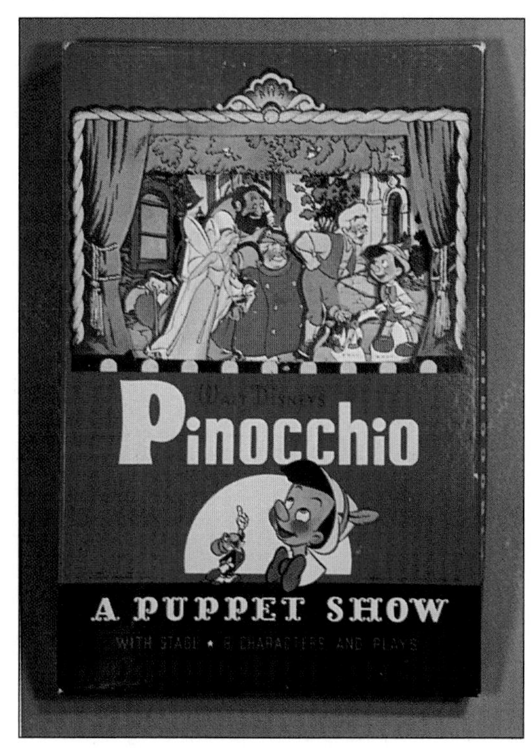

Walt Disney's Pinocchio "A Puppet Show" with stage, eight characters and plays, manufactured by Whitman, ©Walt Disney Productions, 1939, $175.00 – 300.00.

"Geppetto A Story Paint Book," ©Walt Disney Enterprises, 1939, $65.00 – 95.00.

Figaro and Cleo, A Story Paint Book by Walt Disney, published by Whitman, 1939, $65.00 – 95.00.

The Blue Fairy, A Story Paint Book, ©Walt Disney Enterprises, 1939, $65.00 – 95.00.

Pinocchio Doll by Knickerbocker Toys, 10" doll, ©Walt Disney Enterprises, 1939, $375.00 – 550.00.

J. Worthington Foulfellow and Gideon, A Story Paint Book, ©Walt Disney Ent., $65.00 – 95.00.

Pinocchio, A Story Paint Book, ©Walt Disney Enterprises, 1939, $65.00 – 95.00.

Pinocchio Wood Composition Figure by Multi-wood Products of Chicago, ©Walt Disney Prod. Figure is 5" tall, $75.00 – 150.00.

Walt Disney's Pinocchio Target Game by American Toy Works, ©Walt Disney Prod., 1940, $300.00 – 450.00.

Dart Game Board Target, with all figures inside and stand-up target stands (missing dart gun), $300.00 – 450.00.

Geppetto Wood Composition Figure by Multi-products, ©W.D.P., 1949, $125.00 – 200.00.

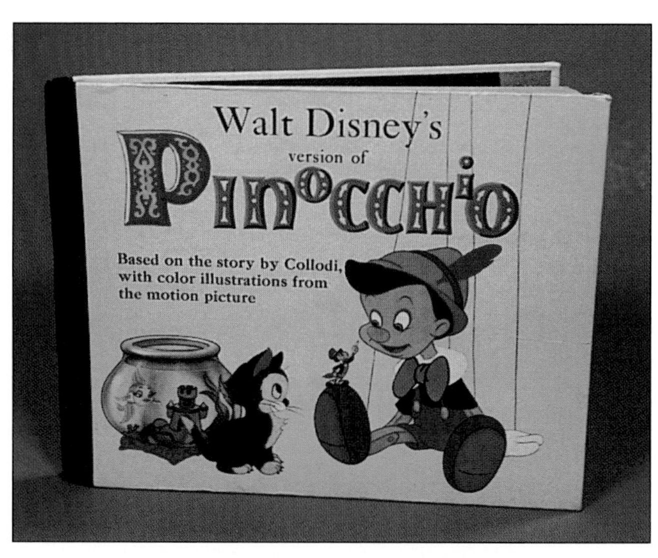

Walt Disney's Version of Pinocchio Storybook, 1940. Featuring full color pictures, $75.00 – 125.00.

Jiminy Cricket Bank by Crown Toy and Novelty, ©W.D.P., 1939, $250.00 – 400.00.

Walt Disney's Pinocchio Fisher-Price Pull Toy, with bell-ringing Pinocchio action, ©Walt Disney Prod. 1940, $375.00 – 600.00.

Pinocchio's Blue Fairy French Postcard, ©Walt Disney, 1939, $35.00 – 50.00.

Pinocchio Riding a Turtle Bank by Crown Toy and Novelty, ©Walt Disney Enterprises, 1939. An extremely rare Pinocchio Bank version, $400.00 – 575.00.

Walt Disney's Pinocchio Storybook, ©Walt Disney Prod., 1940, $45.00 – 75.00.

Detail of Box Lid for "Pinocchio The Merry Puppet Game" by Milton Bradley, 1939, $150.00 – 250.00.
See other photos on page 128.

Jiminy Cricket Wood Composition Figure by Multi Wood Prods. of Chicago, ©Walt Disney Productions, 1940. Note handcarved-looking details and coloring, although this was a factory produced piece, $150.00 – 250.00.

"Jiminy Cricket A Story Paint Book" ©Walt Disney, 1939, $65.00 – 95.00.

Giant 7" Pinocchio Wood Composition Figure by Multi-wood Products of Chicago. ©Walt Disney Prods., 1940, $200.00 – 275.00.

Pinocchio and Jiminy Cricket Wood and Composition Dolls by Ideal Toy and Novelty, ©Walt Disney Prod., 1939, $650.00 – 1,000.00 pair.

Walt Disney's Pinocchio Lobby Card, re-release, ©Walt Disney Prod., 1940s, $65.00 – 90.00.

Pinocchio Framed Litho Print from original release of movie, ©Walt Disney Ent., 1939, $200.00 – 350.00.

Pinocchio French Clay Composition Wind-up, manufactured by "Les Jouets Creation, Paris" shown with rare original box, 1939, $950.00 – 1,200.00.

Pinocchio by Walt Disney. Wood Composition Doll manufactured by Ideal Toy and Novelty 1939 – 1940. Shown with original box, $600.00 – 850.00.

Walt Disney's Pinocchio Picture Book, Published by Grosset and Dunlap, ©Walt Disney Enterprises, 1939, $145.00 – 195.00.

Pinocchio Composition Wind-up Walking Doll, probably French, circa 1939, $300.00 – 475.00.

Pinocchio Wind-up Walker Toy, manufactured by Louis Marx, ©Walt Disney Enterprises, $375.00 – 600.00.

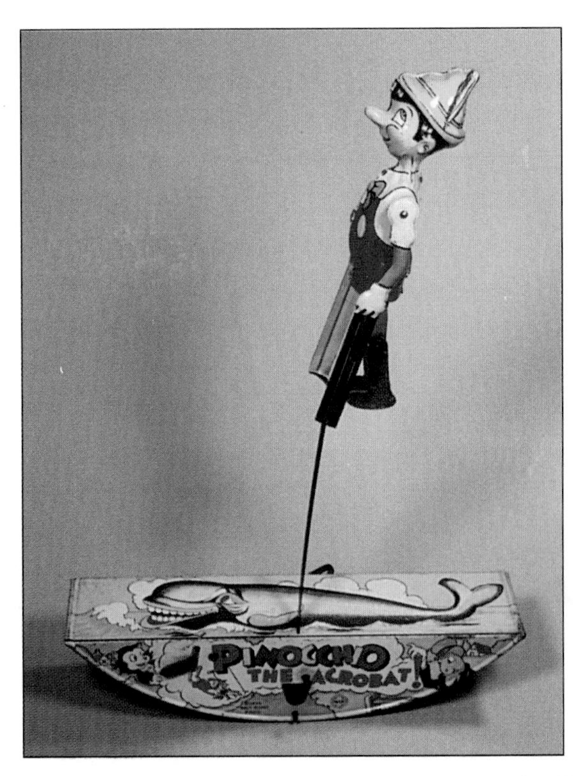

"Pinocchio the Acrobat" Wind-up Action Toy by Louis Marx, ©Walt Disney Productions, 1940, $650.00 – 1,000.00.

Pinocchio Picture Puzzle by Whitman, ©Walt Disney, 1939, $60.00 – 95.00.

Screen Romances Magazine, Jan. 1940 with Pinocchio cover and Disney Studio Pinocchio story inside, $50.00 – 75.00.

Walt Disney's Pinocchio Picture Puzzles, 1939. Boxed set of two puzzles by Whitman, $150.00 – 225.00.

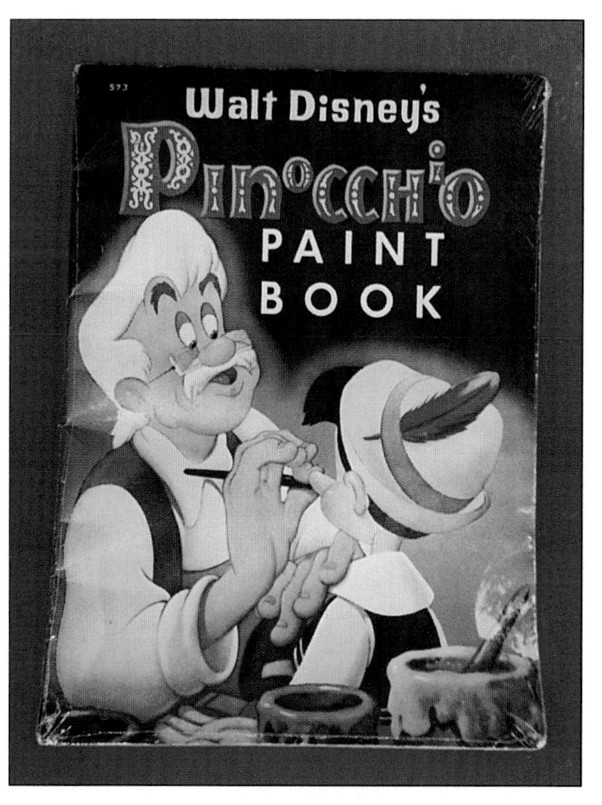

Walt Disney's Pinocchio Paint Book, Giant Paper Back Coloring Book, Whitman, 1939, $100.00 – 140.00.

Walt Disney's Pinocchio The Merry Puppet Game by Milton-Bradley, 1939, $150.00 – 250.00.

"Walt Disney Tells The Story of Pinocchio" small Paperback Storybook, ©Walt Disney Prod., 1939, $75.00 – 100.00.

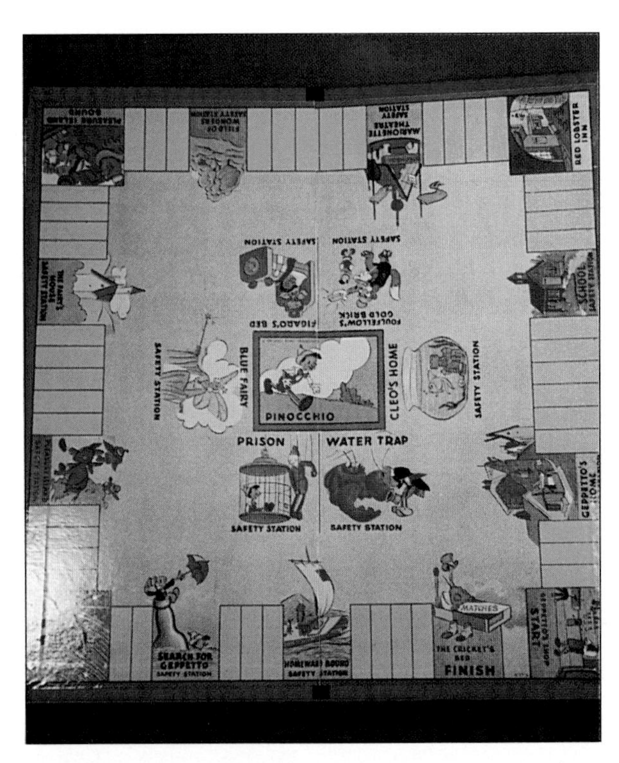

Game Board for boxed Pinocchio Game shown above.

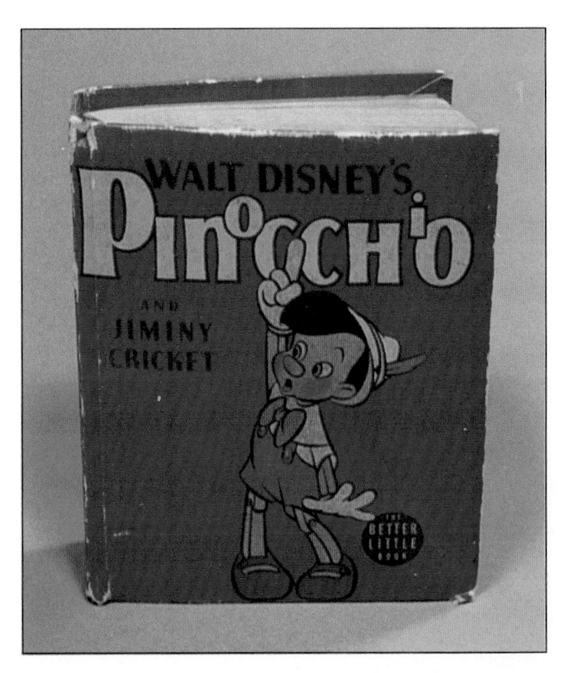

Walt Disney's Pinocchio and Jiminy Cricket, published by Better Little Books, ©Walt Disney, $50.00 – 75.00.

Walt Disney's Bambi Stuffed Toy, 6" with Steiff button and tag, by Steiff of Germany, ©Walt Disney Productions, $125.00 – 175.00.

Bambi Large Ceramic Character Figure by American Pottery, ©Walt Disney, 1940s, $125.00 – 175.00.

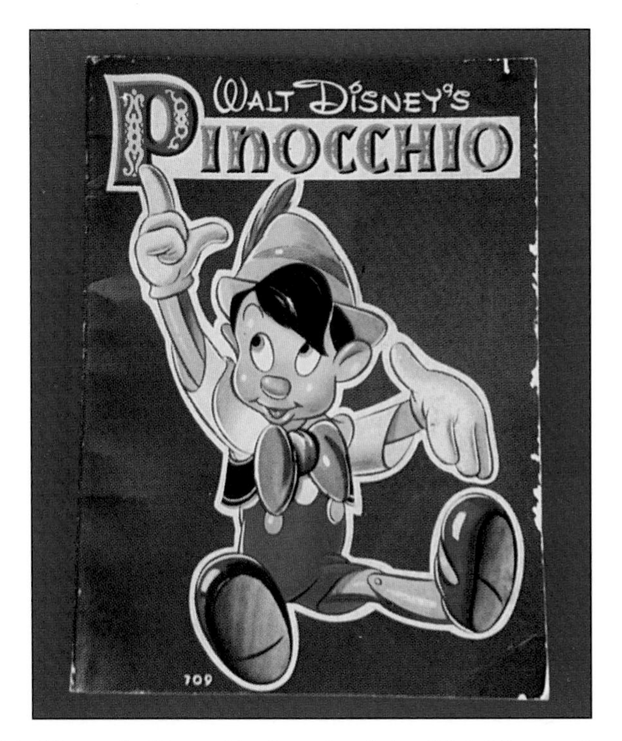

Walt Disney's Pinocchio Storybook by Walt Disney Prod., 1939, $75.00 – 125.00.

Thumper and His Girlfriend Glazed Ceramic Figures by American Pottery Co., ©Walt Disney, 1940s, $60.00 – 85.00.

Baby Dumbo Ceramic Figure by American Pottery, ©Walt Disney Prod., 1940s, $125.00 – 175.00.

Elmer the Elephant Bisque Figure, ©Walt Disney, 1930s. Made in Japan. Figure is a small bank. Rare, $250.00 – 400.00.

Walt Disney's Cinderella Cloth Faced Character Doll with ribbon banner and yarn hair, ©Walt Disney Prod., circa 1950, $300.00 – 450.00.

Joe Carioca French Wind-up Composition Toy, circa early 1940s. From "Three Caballeros" Cartoon Short, ©Walt Disney Prod., $300.00 – 500.00.

Walt Disney's Cinderella Watch, with three changeable bands in original display case, $75.00 – 150.00.

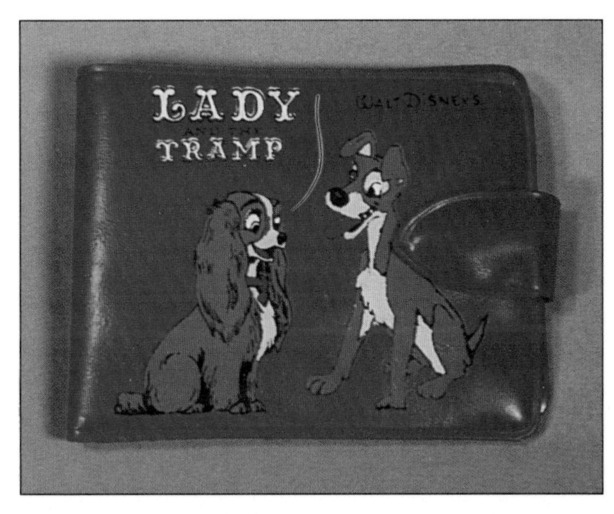

Lady and The Tramp Child's Plastic Wallet, ©Walt Disney Productions, 1950s, $25.00 – 40.00.

Walt Disney's "Lady" Rolling Hard Plastic Toy, Doll, and Platform Pull-along, circa 1950s. Toy is designed as a Doll or a Platform toy with a pull cord. $200.00 – 300.00.

Walt Disney's Dancing Cinderella and Prince Hard Plastic Wind-up Toy, with original box, $150.00 – 250.00.

HANNA-BARBERA TOYS

The animated cartoons of perhaps no other studio are more recognized by the world's present-day population than those of Hanna-Barbera. The cartoons of this studio are just old enough to have been loved by today's aging baby boomers who watched them as children and who now enjoy watching them be introduced to their own children who sit mesmerized in front of the television watching the likes of George Jetson and Fred Flintstone.

And that remarkable southern drawl of one Huckleberry Hound complimented by the continual antics of one eternally hungry Yogi Bear are cartoon trademarks that have now touched at least three generations! Ask anyone who loves cartoons if they are fans of the creations of Hanna-Barbera and the answer will be one of resounding approval. The fantastically popular 1960s creations of this studio are to that decade what Walt Disney cartoons were to the 1930s.

Certainly the most popular early 1960s cartoons were those starring the likes of Huckleberry Hound, Yogi Bear, and Quick Draw McGraw. With the introduction of their Flintstones series, which bears the honor of being America's first prime time evening aired cartoon series, Hanna-Barbera scored yet another animation hit.

It is interesting to note the creativity of Hanna-Barbera with its series development during the 1960s. On one hand, they introduced America to the animated prehistoric caveman era with Fred Flintstone and Barney Rubble working at a stone quarry and riding around on top of dinosaurs like Dino, while at nearly the same time, they were producing the far-out futuristic series of the Jetsons which capitalized on the 1960s craze with science fiction, the future, and outer space. It is noteworthy that this studio was able to capture a nation's imagination at both ends of the human time line with characters which appealed to all ages, adults and children alike. Whether it was flying saucers dashing about the galaxy piloted by space age children, or housewives who lived next door to one another in neighboring caves, both the Jetsons and the Flintstones captured the human essence of all of us.

As a child, this author's most adored toy was one in the likeness of a Hanna-Barbera character. Quick Draw McGraw's Mexican donkey sidekick was Baba Looey, and for Christmas 1960, I was given a plush and vinyl likeness of the little guy who would sleep with me in bed for the next four or five years. I am not sure to this day why I asked Santa for Baba Looey and not one of the more popular Huckleberry Hound or Yogi Bear toys that were available. I am sure I would have liked them just as much. But for some childish reason, the donkey was the toy I had to have, and he became a treasured childhood friend.

It seems, at the time, Hanna-Barbera cartoons were shown all the time. You could catch new series cartoons in the evening, reruns after school, and certainly there had to be plenty of Saturday morning viewings. I am certain that not a day went by (except for Sundays) that the beloved cartoons by this studio weren't served up regularly to cartoon-watching kids and parents alike. Hanna-Barbera characters were the stars of the 1960s. There is no doubt about that!

So, although toys licensed by this studio to the toy manufacturers may not have brought the staggering dollar amounts at auctions in past years that vintage Disneyana toys have, the Hanna-Barbera character toy designs are certainly no less loved by today's baby boomers. And whether it's Quick Draw or Huckleberry, Atom Ant or Magilla Gorilla, George Jetson or Fred Flintstone, the characters of Hanna-Barbera have certainly worked their way into the American mainstream over the past three decades and into the hearts of millions of young people.

Hanna-Barbera collecting is another area of animation/cartoon collecting that has not yet earned its due respect. But that day is coming.

The value of Hanna-Barbera toys today is that they dominate their era. Disney had a golden age of character merchandising in the 1930s, and Warner Brothers character toys came into their own in the 1940s and 1950s. Hanna-Barbera toys represent the very best of cartoon merchandising for the decades of the 1960s and 1970s.

For the novice cartoon character collector, collecting toys from this studio is a great place to start. For the advanced collector, there were so many characters introduced by Hanna-Barbera in the 1960s and 1970s that, like Disney, it's almost impossible to collect them all.

For new and experienced collectors alike, collecting Hanna-Barbera character toys is exciting, challenging, colorful, and potentially profitable with the toys on the secondary market today usually quite a bargain compared to other cartoon toys.

For avid fans of Huckleberry and Yogi, this area is a great place to start!

Huckleberry Hound Stuffed Plush Toy, ©Hanna-Barbera, circa 1960s, $60.00 – 95.00.

Yogi Bear Plush Toy, ©Hanna-Barbera. Shown with rare original box, 1960s, $200.00 – 400.00.

Hanna-Barbera's "Yogi Bear No Picnic" Storybook published by Top Top Tales, $12.00 – 20.00.

Yogi Bear Lamp with original shade, ©Hanna-Barbera, 1960s, $150.00 – 275.00.

Huckleberry Hound Western Game manufactured by Milton Bradley of Springfield, Mass., and copyright Hanna-Barbera, $45.00 – 75.00.

Game Board for Huckleberry Hound Western Game pictured above.

Hanna-Barbera's Huckleberry Hound Giant Storybook, large size format, ©Hanna-Barbera, circa 1960s, $15.00 – 25.00.

Hanna-Barbera's Huckleberry Hound, A Whitman Comic Book, circa 1960s. Contains comic book layout stories inside, $10.00 – 20.00.

Yogi Bear and Friends Lunch Box by Aladdin, ©Hanna-Barbera, 1960s. Pictures Mr. Ranger chasing Yogi and friends, $75.00 – 100.00.

Yogi Bear and Friends Lunch Box, reverse design.

Huckleberry Hound and His Friends Lunch Box manufactured by Aladdin, ©Hanna-Barbera, 1960s. Shown with original Thermos and in excellent condition, $85.00 – 125.00.

Quick Draw McGraw and Friends Lunch Box design on reverse.

Yogi Bear Game by The Milton Bradley Co., ©Hanna-Barbera, 1960s, $40.00 – 65.00.

Game Board for Yogi Bear Game pictured above.

Huckleberry Hound and Yogi Bear Airplane, made in Japan. Copyright Hanna-Barbera, 1960s, $375.00 – 550.00.

Yogi Bear Child's Plastic Cup, ©Hanna-Barbera, 1960s, $18.00 – 30.00.

Huckleberry Hound "Bumps" Game by Transogram, ©Hanna-Barbera Productions, 1960s. Very desirable boxed game, $125.00 – 175.00.

Huckleberry Hound "Bumps" Game, Game Board and Spinner with Playing Pieces pictured.

Detail of Huckleberry Hound "Bumps" Game pictured on previous page.

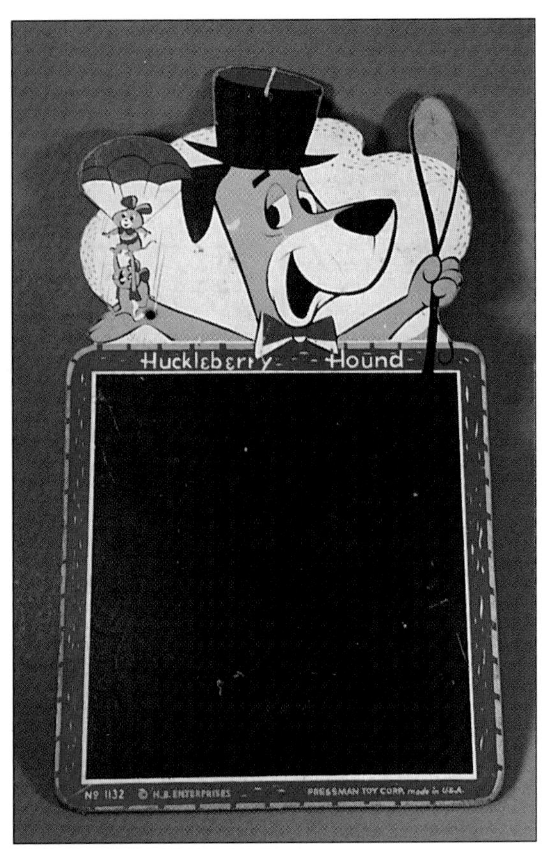

Huckleberry Hound Chalk Board by Pressman Toy Corp., 1960s, ©Hanna-Barbera, $35.00 – 50.00.

Huckleberry Hound Cartoon Kit, 1962, by Hanna-Barbera Productions. One of the very earliest of all Colorforms toys, $125.00 – 175.00.

Quick Draw McGraw and The Flintstones Card Games, ©Hanna-Barbera, 1960s, $15.00 – 20.00 each.

Kenner's Give-A-Show Projector Set, with cartoon pictures, ©Hanna-Barbera, 1960s, $75.00 – 125.00.

Inside box view of Give-A-Show Projector.

Huckleberry Hound Character Plaque, ©Hanna-Barbera, $75.00 – 100.00.

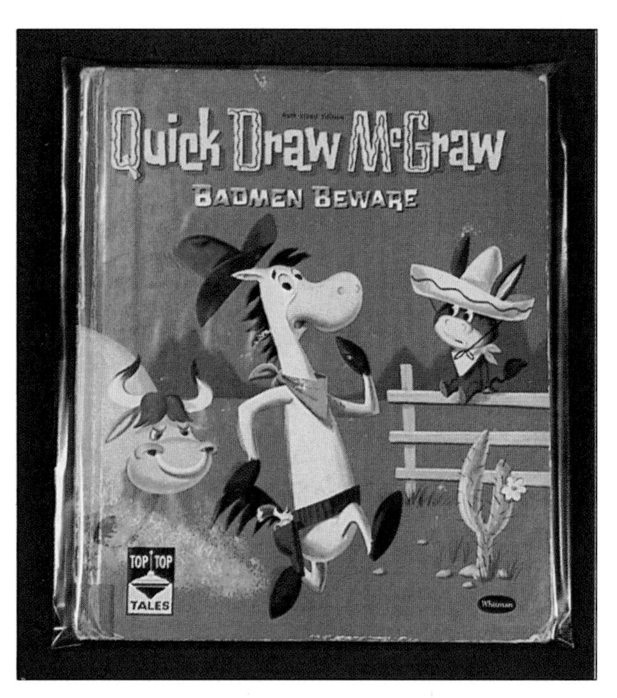

"Quick Draw McGraw Badmen Beware," Whitman Publishing Top Tales, 1960s, $12.00 – 20.00.

Yogi Bear Little Golden Book by Whitman, ©Hanna-Barbera, 1960s, $10.00 – 15.00.

Yogi Bear and Boo-Boo Coat Rack, ©Hanna-Barbera, 1960s, $75.00 – 125.00.

Yogi Bear's Favorite Activities Fun Book, ©Hanna-Barbera, recent, $5.00 – 10.00.

Flintstones Cut-ups Card Game, ©Hanna-Barbera, 1960s. Showing oil cloth game board, $75.00 – 95.00.

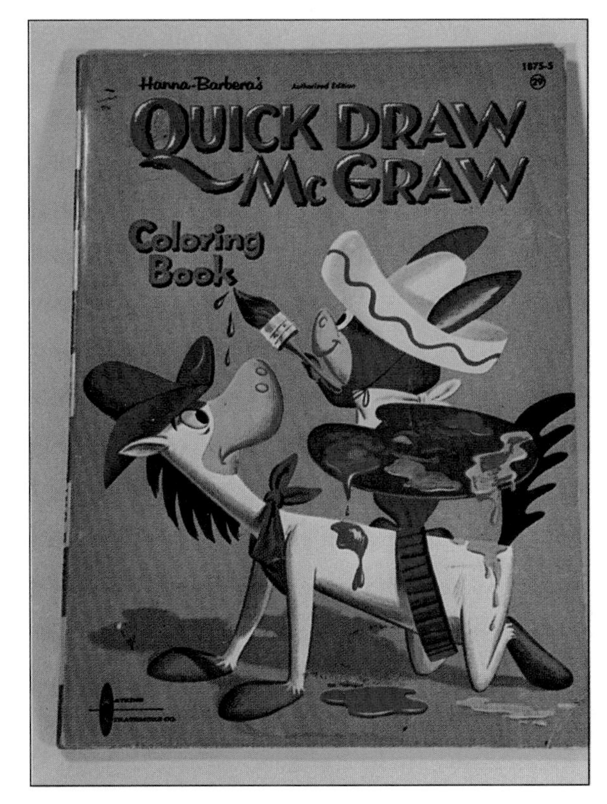

Hanna-Barbera's Quick Draw McGraw Coloring Book, 1960s, $25.00 – 50.00.

Flintstones Cut-ups Game, reverse side of playing board picturing Barney and Betty Rubble.

Fred Flintstone Plaster Composition Bank, ©Hanna-Barbera, 1960s, $75.00 – 125.00.

Yogi Bear Wipe off Coloring Cloth with Crayons, ©Hanna-Barbera, circa 1960s, $20.00 – 35.00.

Huckleberry Hound and Yogi Bear Figures Rubber Toys, ©Hanna-Barbera, 1960s, $20.00 – 35.00 each.

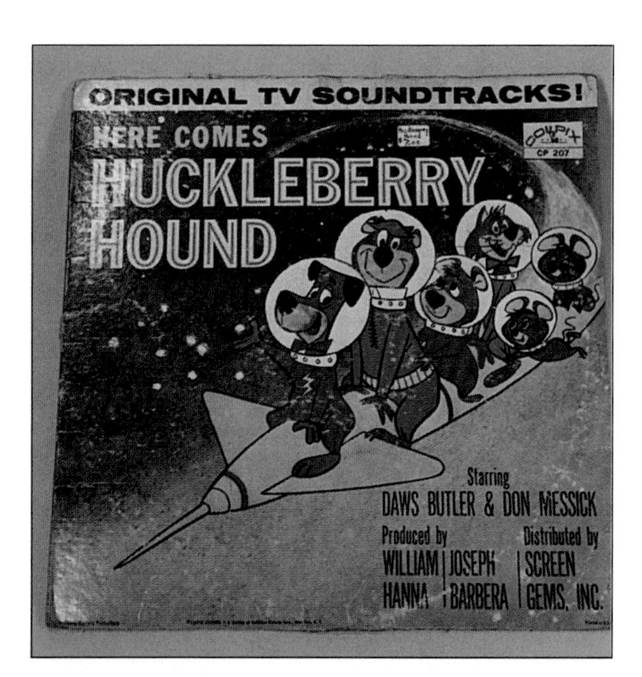

Huckleberry Hound original TV Sound Track Record, ©Hanna-Barbera and Screen Gems, 1960s, $20.00 – 35.00.

Huckleberry Hound Happy Birthday Napkins, ©Hanna-Barbera Productions, 1959, $20.00 – 35.00.

Yogi Bear Plastic Bubble Pipe, ©Hanna-Barbera, 1960s, $15.00 – 25.00.

Yogi Bear and Huckleberry Hound Card Games, ©Hanna-Barbera, 1960s, $12.00 – 20.00 each.

Mechanical Wilma Flintstone Wind-up Tin and Celluloid Tricycle by Line Mar, Japan, ©Hanna-Barbera. Shown with original box, $450.00 – 700.00.

Fred Flintstone and Daughter Pebbles Hand Puppets, ©Hanna-Barbera, 1960s, $35.00 – 50.00 each.

Flintstones Pebbles Vinyl Doll, ©Hanna-Barbera, recent, $10.00 – 15.00.

Flintstones Pebbles Vinyl Doll, with original clothes, ©Hanna-Barbera, $20.00 – 35.00.

Barney Rubble Stuffed Plush Character from The Flintstones, ©Hanna-Barbera, circa 1960s, $40.00 – 65.00.

Dino the Dinosaur Character from The Flintstones, ©Hanna-Barbera, probably 1970s, $35.00 – 55.00.

Dino the Dinosaur Stuffed Character Doll from The Flintstones, ©Hanna-Barbera, $35.00 – 60.00.

Yogi Bear Plush Toy, with original tag, ©Hanna-Barbera, $25.00 – 45.00.

The Jetsons Game by Milton Bradley, ©Hanna-Barbera, 1960s, $45.00 – 75.00.

Betty Rubble Line Mar Wind-up Flintstones Character Car, ©Hanna-Barbera, $400.00 – 675.00.

Fred and Barney Flintstones Car, ©Hanna-Barbera, $40.00 – 65.00.

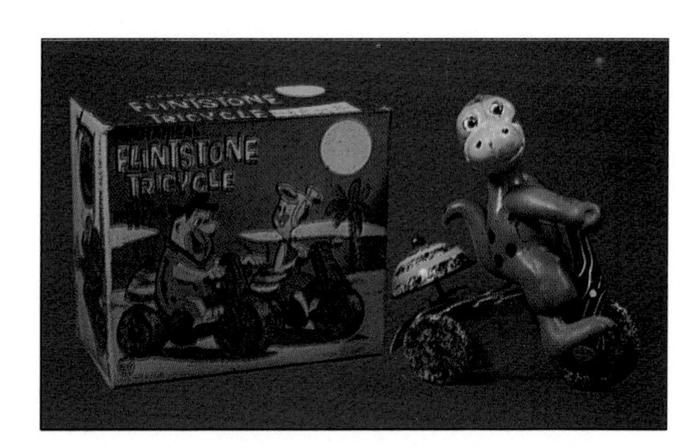

Mechanical Flintstones Tricycle with Dino by Line Mar, ©Hanna-Barbera. Rare wind-up with celluloid figure, $600.00 – 900.00.

Hanna-Barbera's The Jetsons "Hopping George" in rare original box, manufactured by Line Mar Toys, ©Hanna-Barbera, $750.00 – 1,000.00.

Astro the Dog from "The Jetsons" Hanna-Barbera Character Wind-up by Line Mar, $400.00 – 575.00.

Top Cat Hanna-Barbera Character Book by Whitman Publishing Big Golden Books, ©Hanna-Barbera, 1960s, $20.00 – 30.00.

Jinks the Cat Frame Tray Puzzle with Pixie and Dixie, Hanna-Barbera, 1960s, $20.00 – 30.00.

"The Jetsons, The Birthday Surprise" Storybook, ©Hanna-Barbera, 1960s, $10.00 – 20.00.

The Jetsons Frame Tray Puzzle, showing George Jetson and Elroy, ©Hanna-Barbera, 1960s, $25.00 – 45.00.

Hanna-Barbera Bubble Club Character Containers featuring Peter Potamus on left, $15.00 – 25.00 each.

Quick Draw McGraw Character Wall Plaque, ©Hanna-Barbera Prod., $75.00 – 100.00.

Dino the Flintstones Dinosaur Vinyl Character Toy, ©Hanna-Barbera, $25.00 – 35.00.

Quick Draw McGraw Frame Tray Puzzle, ©Hanna-Barbera Prod., 1960s, $20.00 – 30.00.

Huckleberry Hound and Quick Draw McGraw Wastebasket, 1960s. Rare in such great condition. Featuring all of the popular 1960s Hanna-Barbera characters, ©Hanna-Barbera, $175.00 – 300.00. Reverse side is shown in the photo below.

Huckleberry Hound Soap Toy and Bank, ©Hanna-Barbera, 1960s, $25.00 – 35.00.

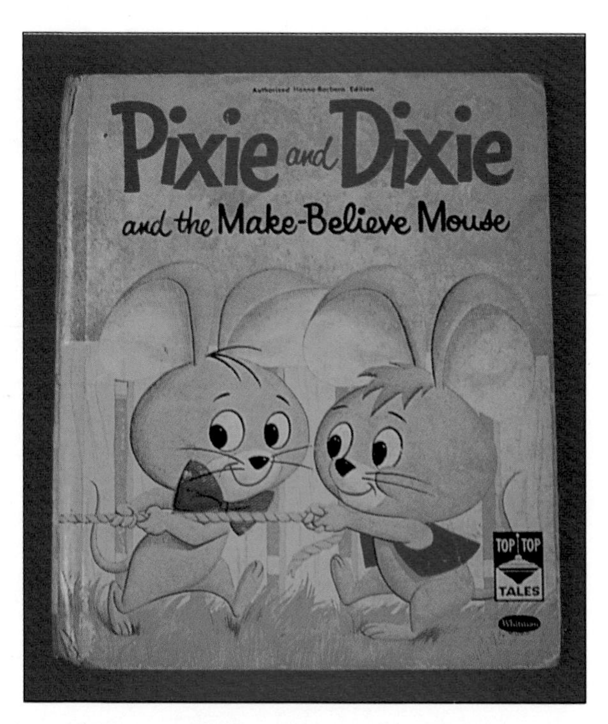

Pixie and Dixie and The Make-Believe Mouse, Top Top Tales by Whitman, ©Hanna-Barbera, $15.00 – 25.00.

Hopping Barney Rubble from The Flintstones by Line Mar with original box, ©Hanna-Barbera, $650.00 – 900.00.

Barney Rubble Tin Flintstones Character Wind-up by Line Mar, ©Hanna-Barbera, 1960s, $500.00 – 750.00.

The Flintstones Stoneage Game by Transogram, ©Hanna-Barbera, 1960s, $75.00 – 125.00.

Opened Game Board for Flintstones Game above.

Fred Flintstone Push Puppet and Trapeze Toys, ©Hanna-Barbera, 1960s, $50.00 – 75.00 each.

Magilla Gorilla and Secret Squirrel Hanna-Barbera Character Push Puppets, plastic, ©Hanna-Barbera, 1960s, $50.00 – 75.00.

Fred Flintstone's Bedrock Band Tin Battery Operated Toy, ©Hanna-Barbera Prod., 1960s, $750.00 – 1,000.00 each.

Pebbles Flintstone Little Golden Book by Whitman, ©Hanna-Barbera, 1960s, $12.00 – 20.00.

Flintstones Character Vinyl Doll, ©Hanna-Barbera, 1960s, $65.00 – 95.00.

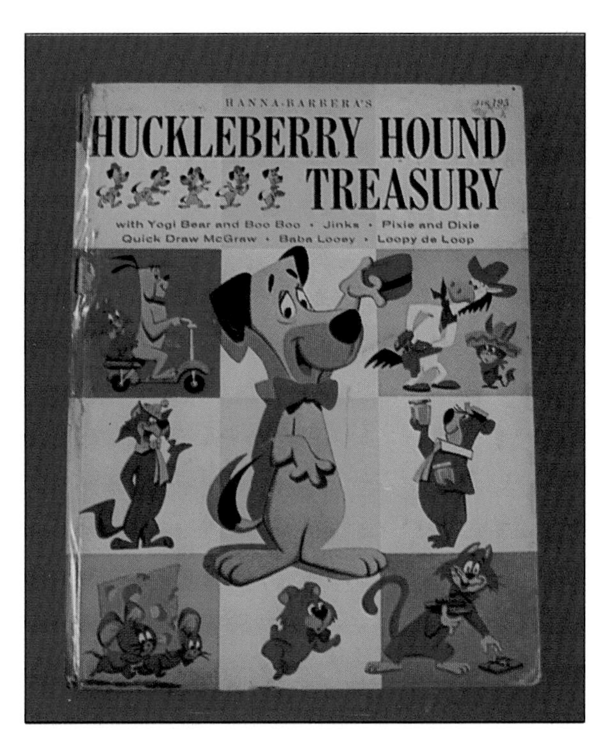

Hanna-Barbera's Huckleberry Hound Storybook Treasury, 1960s, $20.00 – 30.00.

Large Cloth and Vinyl Flintstones Character Doll, ©Hanna-Barbera, 1960s, $125.00 – 175.00.

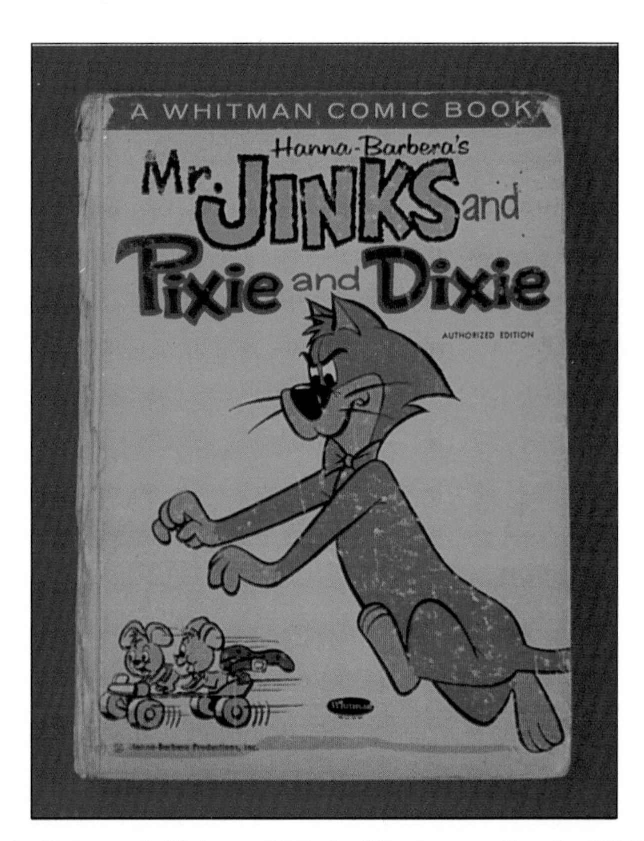

Mr. Jinks and Pixie and Dixie, Hardcover Comic, Whitman Comic Book, ©Hanna-Barbera, 1960s, $18.00 – 30.00.

Snooper and Blabber and Quick Draw Comic Book by Whitman, ©Hanna-Barbera, 1960s, $18.00 – 30.00.

Huckleberry Hound Helps a Pal, Top Top Tales Book by Whitman, ©Hanna-Barbera, $15.00 – 20.00.

Yogi Bear Whitman Hardcover Comic, ©Hanna-Barbera, 1960s, $18.00 – 30.00.

"Huckleberry Hound Builds A House" Little Golden Books, ©Hanna-Barbera, $12.00 – 18.00.

Fred Flintstone Character Clock, 12" tall glazed ceramic figure, ©Hanna-Barbera, $125.00 – 200.00.

Hanna-Barbera's "Yogi Bear A Christmas Visit" Little Golden Book, ©Hanna-Barbera, $12.00 – 20.00.

The Rubbles and Bamm-Bamm Problem Present, published by Whitman Tell-A-Tale Books, ©Hanna-Barbera 1960s, $12.00 – 20.00.

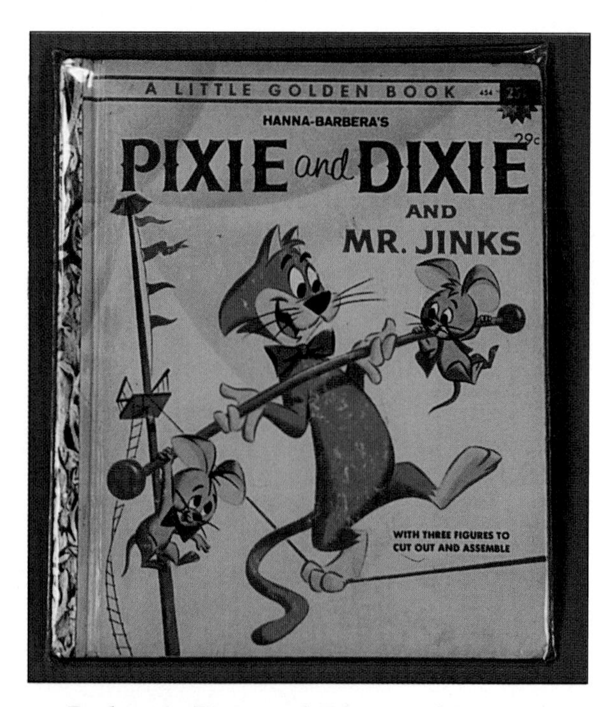

Hanna-Barbera's Pixie and Dixie and Mr. Jinks Little Golden Book, $12.00 – 18.00.

Flintstone Flivver by Line Mar of Japan, ©Hanna-Barbera, 1960s, $600.00 – 950.00.

Fred Flintstone Tin Wind-up by Line Mar, ©Hanna-Barbera, $500.00 – 750.00.

Fred Flintstone Character Toy Riding Giant Dino the Dinosaur, 1960s, $1,000.00 – 1,500.00.

Yogi Bear House Slipper Boots, in original box, ©Hanna-Barbera, 1960s, $125.00 – 175.00.

Detail of Yogi Bear House Slipper Boots box art.

Huckleberry Hound Undercover Police Dog Paperback Storybook, ©Hanna-Barbera, 1960s, $10.00 – 20.00.

The Flintstones, The Case Of The Missing Peanut Butter, paperback, ©Hanna-Barbera, 1960s, $10.00 – 20.00.

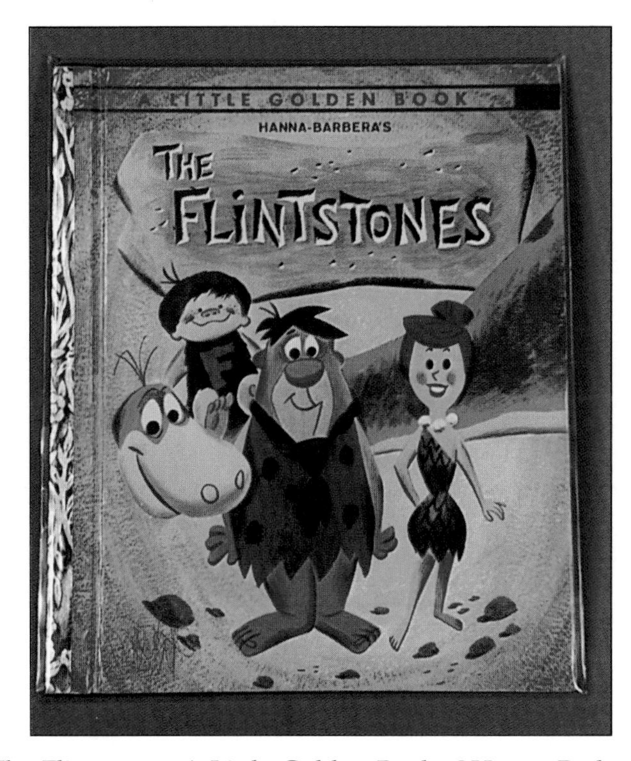

The Flintstones, A Little Golden Book, ©Hanna-Barbera, $8.00 – 15.00.

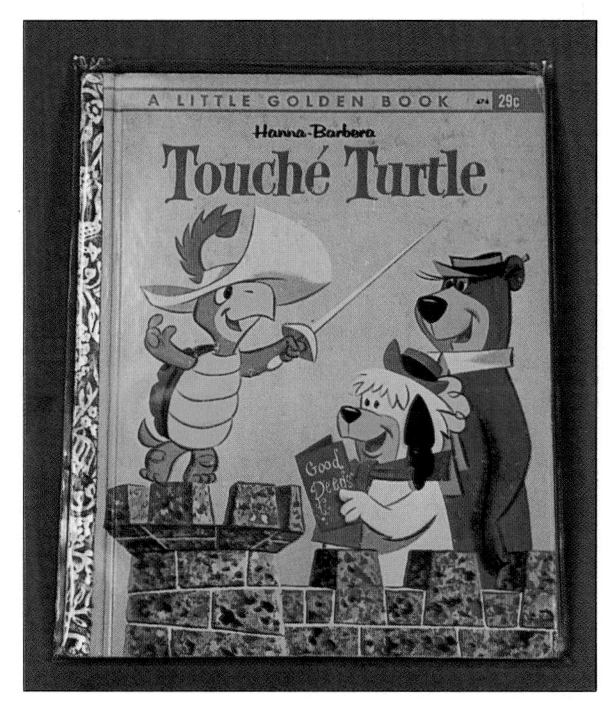

Hanna-Barbera's Touche´ Turtle, Little Golden Book, $8.00 – 15.00.

The Flintstones Lunch Box by Aladdin Industries, ©Hanna-Barbera Productions, 1962. Perfect example of vintage Flintstones character design, $75.00 – 100.00.

Flintstones and Dino Lunch Box reverse design.

Huckleberry Hound and Yogi Bear View-Master Cartoon Favorites by GAF, ©Hanna-Barbera, $10.00 – 15.00.

Quick Draw McGraw View-Master Cartoon Favorites by GAF, ©Hanna-Barbera, $10.00 – 15.00.

Jellystone Park Yogi Bear Plate, ©Hanna-Barbera, $20.00 – 45.00.

Flintstones Pebbles Plastic Cereal Bowl, ©Hanna-Barbera, 1960s, $15.00 – 30.00.

Pebbles and Bamm-Bamm Flintstones Children Character Dolls, shown wearing original clothes, ©Hanna-Barbera, $135.00 – 275.00 pair.

Flintstones Pebbles Vinyl Toy, ©Hanna-Barbera, $15.00 – 25.00.

Wally Gator Bubble Club Bath Soap and Toy Figure, ©Hanna-Barbera, $20.00 – 40.00.

Spouty Whale Flintstones Fun Bath "From The Peter Potamus Show," ©Hanna-Barbera, $20.00 – 40.00.

Cartoonist Stamp Set Featuring Quick Draw McGraw, Yogi Bear, and Huckleberry Hound Stamps, ©Hanna-Barbera, 1960s, $75.00 – 125.00.

Jetsons Game Board by Milton Bradley, copyright Hanna-Barbera, 1960s. Value for board (as shown) only, $20.00 – 30.00.

Hanna-Barbera "Mush Mouse" series Character Toys, featuring hard-to-find character collectibles from this studio, $35.00 – 70.00 pair.

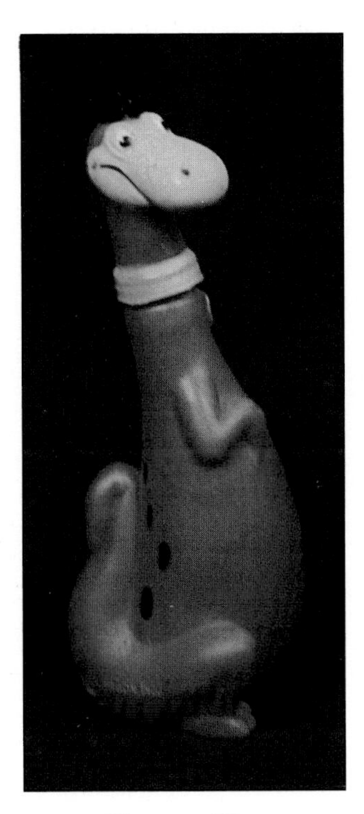

Dino the Dinosaur Plastic Figure, approx. 6" tall, ©Hanna-Barbera, $15.00 – 25.00.

Hanna-Barbera's The Flintstones, A Whitman Comic Book, 1960s. Contains comic book format story inside, $15.00 – 25.00.

Flintstones Plastic Child's Plate, ©Hanna-Barbera, 1960s, $25.00 – 45.00.

Yogi Bear Lunch Box, manufactured by Aladdin Industries of Nashville, Tenn., ©Hanna-Barbera, $35.00 – 65.00.

Kong Phooey, Hanna-Barbera Thermos Lunch Box, 1960s, $40.00 – 70.00.

Pebbles Flintstone Frame Tray Puzzle, ©Hanna-Barbera, 1960s, $15.00 – 25.00.

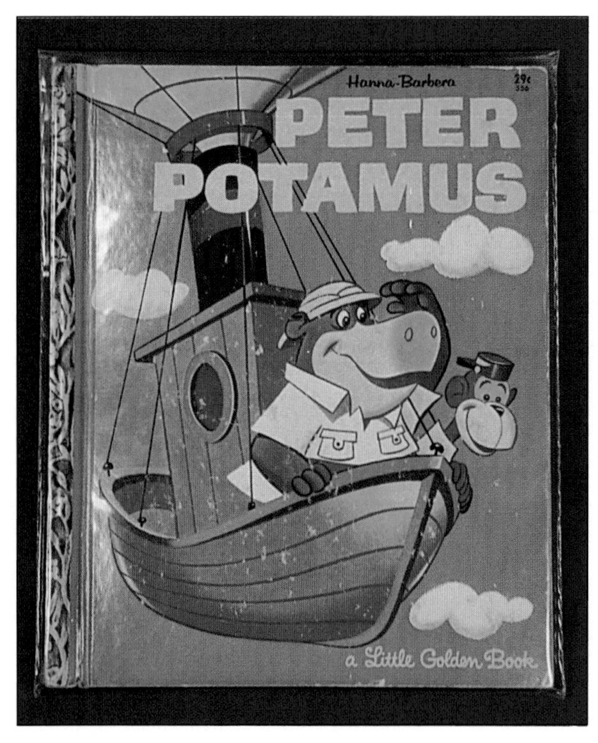

Hanna-Barbera Character Peter Potamus Little Golden Book, ©Hanna-Barbera, $8.00 – 12.00.

Flintstone's "Fred Yabba Dabba Doo!" Alarm Clock, ©Hanna-Barbera, $35.00 – 65.00.

Flintstones Character Thermos Bottle, ©Hanna-Barbera, $25.00 – 45.00.

Flintstones Fun Bath Bathtub Floater Toy featuring "new" duck character Yakky Doodle. Advertising collar around Yakky is particularly colorful. Picturing all the popular Hanna-Barbera characters, $40.00 – 65.00.

Huckleberry Hound and Yogi Bear 78rpm Golden Record, ©Hanna-Barbera, 1960s, $10.00 – 20.00.

Hanna-Barbera "The Jetsons" A Little Golden Book, circa 1960s, $8.00 – 12.00.

Hanna-Barbera Atom Ant Soap Toy, 1960s, $15.00 – 30.00.

"Loopy De Loop Goes West," Little Golden Book of Hanna-Barbera Adventure Cat with the French Accent, $8.00 – 12.00.

Hanna-Barbera Witch Character Soap Container with Screw-off Head, $20.00 – 35.00.

"The Flintstones Game...The Game That Rocked Bedrock," circa 1960s, ©Hanna-Barbera, $65.00 – 100.00.

Pebbles and Bamm-Bamm Hanna-Barbera Character Lunch Box by Aladdin, $40.00 – 75.00.

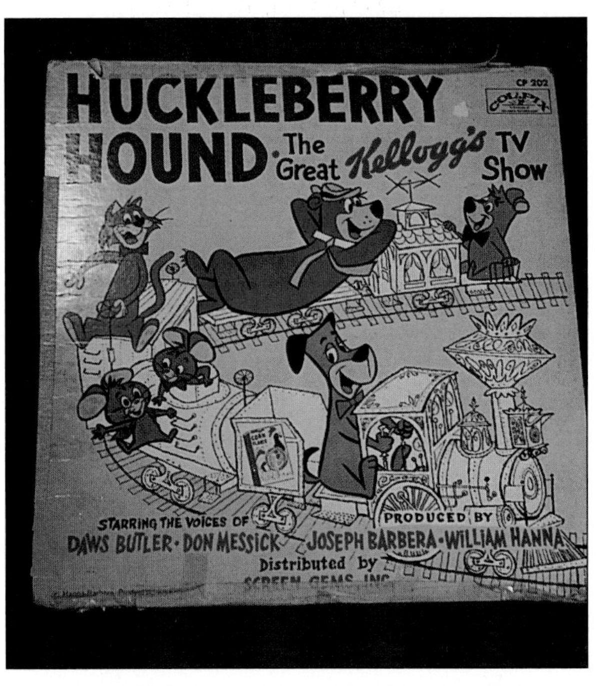

Huckleberry Hound The Great Kellogg's TV Show Record Album, 1960s, $10.00 – 20.00.

Hanna-Barbera's Top Cat Character Frame Tray Puzzle, 1960s, ©Hanna-Barbera, $15.00 – 25.00.

Yogi Bear Mug, ©Hanna-Barbera, 1960s, $20.00 – 30.00.

Hanna-Barbera Figural Bath Soap Containers, ©Hanna-Barbera. Pictured here are Ricochet Rabbit and Mush Mouse, $20.00 – 45.00.

Yogi Bear Child's Transistor Radio, ©Hanna-Barbera, $25.00 – 40.00.

Baba Looey and Quick Draw McGraw Bubble Bath Toys with bank slots on top, circa 1960s. Both copyright Hanna-Barbera, $25.00 – 40.00 each.

Yogi Bear Ceramic Figure, ©Hanna-Barbera, circa 1960s, $35.00 – 55.00.

Yogi Bear Bubble Bath Toy and Bank, ©Hanna-Barbera, 1960s, $25.00 – 40.00.

Hanna-Barbera Character Bath Soap Toys with Bank Character Heads, 1960s. Figures pictured are Punkin Puss and Top Cat, $20.00 – 35.00 each.

Hanna-Barbera's Penelope Pitstop Frame Tray Puzzle, $15.00 – 25.00.

Huckleberry Hound and Auggie Doggie Bubble Bath Containers, ©Hanna-Barbera, 1960s, $20.00 – 35.00 each.

Flintstones Characters Frame Tray Puzzle, ©Hanna-Barbera Prod., $20.00 – 30.00.

Hanna-Barbera Character Ruff and Reddy Game manufactured by Transogram, ©Hanna-Barbera, 1960s, $50.00 – 85.00.

Detail of Game Board for Ruff and Reddy Game at left.

Fred Flintstone Vinyl Character Doll, ©Hanna-Barbera, $50.00 – 75.00.

Huckleberry Hound Postman Game by Milton Bradley, ©Hanna-Barbera, $40.00 – 65.00.

CARTOON CHARACTER HALL OF FAME

Although the cartoon toys pictured in this chapter were not created by the "big three" of character animation studios, Walt Disney, Warner Brothers, and Hanna-Barbera, they are by no means any less significant. Each of these gigantic studios had extremely impressive decades of moving animated film characters into the popular, mainstream imagination of our culture. For Walt Disney Studios, it was the decade of the 1930s that catapulted it into the limelight with the "Silly Symphonies," "Mickey Mouse Cartoons," "Snow White and the Seven Dwarfs," and "Pinocchio." Although Disney films continued their impressive rise throughout the next two decades, in the 1940s Warner Brothers Cartoons featuring Bugs Bunny, Tweetie and Sylvester, Porky Pig, and Elmer Fudd gave Mickey Mouse and Donald Duck a real run for their money. By the 1950s, both Disney and Warner Brothers were well on their respective ways to becoming lasting creators of classic film animation, and in the 1960s, Hanna-Barbera Studios carved their own animation history niche by moving their impressive animations straight to television without relying upon earlier successes with movie medium experiments as Warner Brothers and Disney had done.

The successes of the major studios often tend to overshadow the significant cartoon creations by smaller studios or simple adaptations of comic strip characters to animation features.

One of the best examples of continually overlooked animation classics are the feature length, made for television "Peanuts" specials. Although the Charles M. Schulz "Peanuts" characters are now world renowned, most people assume it was primarily because of their famous comic strip format. Every generation living today is aware that the television specials featuring "Peanuts" characters during the 1960s and 1970s are what launched them into super-stardom.

Some critics of animation would criticize that the "Peanuts" animated television specials were not terribly sophisticated, with only the simplest movements of the characters and rather plain backgrounds being the order of the day. But it is that simplicity that made the Halloween, Christmas, and Spring specials so unique. Without being overly technical and artistic, the Charlie Brown specials captured the simple warmth and charm of the original comic strips. Watching a Charles Schulz character film special is like watching a moving Sunday color comics page. These specials didn't attempt to compete with Disney, they chose to capture a simplicity that fans of the comic strip would appreciate and children would understand. And their efforts succeeded at both levels.

So, this chapter contains a few of the literally thousands of Peanuts character items that have been licensed in the past 50 years. It is certainly only a sampling. Likewise, the few Betty Boop and Felix the Cat toys pictured are only a tiny introduction as to what is out there for the collector to collect.

Also included in this chapter are recent vintage toys from "The Smurfs" cartoon series and the ever popular "Teenage Mutant Ninja Turtles." These toys are included to represent two powerhouse areas of recent collecting, and there are already scores of collectibles for those who specialize in nothing but these two specialty areas. An important note to collectors of these recent vintage toys is to learn all you can about the secondary market. New Smurf and Ninja Turtle merchandise is still being marketed, so it is important for collectors to know if they are buying something that is brand new, but used, or if it is truly a no longer manufactured piece. Both types of items are collectible, but toys that are still in ready supply should not command prices that out of production pieces do.

As long as film and television studios continue to develop new cartoon characters, there will be a market for the toys inspired by them, both on the active retail market, and when the toys disappear from the toy store shelves, they will amazingly reappear on the secondary market flea market shelves.

Cartoon character toy collecting is a fun and never-ending cycle. The cartoons keep coming and so do the toys!

May the fun of being a child once again never end.

Betty Boop and Bimbo Ceramic Lusterware Ashtray, Japan, 1930s, $175.00 – 300.00.

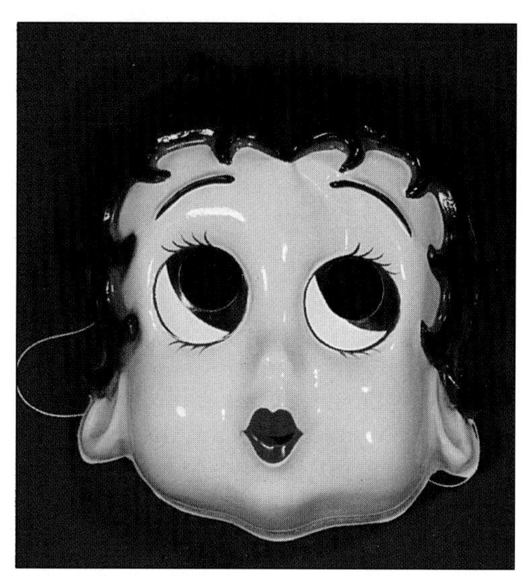

Betty Boop Plastic Costume Mask, date unknown, $35.00 – 65.00.

Scrappy Cartoon Character Bisques from 1930s Cartoon Series, $125.00 – 250.00 pair.

Set of Three Betty Boop Cartoon Characters, ©Max Fleischer, 1930s, $250.00 – 400.00 set of three.

Betty Boop and Bimbo Lusterware Ashtray, glazed ceramic, different version from ashtray at top left, 1930s, $200.00 – 300.00.

Betty Boop Character Musician Bisques featuring Betty with two musical Bimbo figures, $300.00 – 500.00 set of three.

Betty Boop 1930s Character Socks with logo and early Betty Boop Button. Button, $30.00 – 50.00. Socks, $20.00 – 35.00 pair.

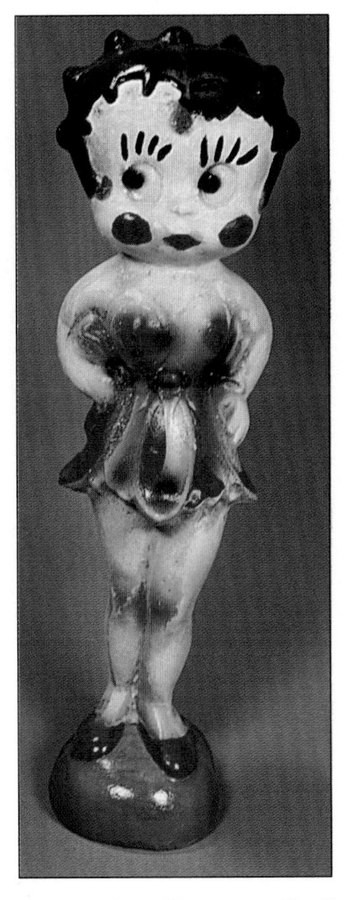

Betty Boop, Max Fleischer Character Chalk Figure, carnival piece, circa 1930s, $75.00 – 125.00.

Betty Boop Character Doll, ©Max Fleischer Studios, recent, $65.00 – 85.00.

Betty Boop Big Dress-up Set by Colorforms, circa 1970s. A later set (recent) but good depiction of Betty and Bimbo, $25.00 – 45.00.

Betty Boop and Bimbo Characters Lusterware Wall Pocket, china glazed ceramic, made in Japan, circa 1930s, $150.00 – 275.00.

Scrappy Cartoon Character Soap in absolute mint condition. A very rare soap figure with all original paint, $125.00 – 200.00.

Flip the Frog, early 1930s Cartoon Character Celluloid figure, 7" tall, $275.00 – 400.00.

Felix the Cat Wood Jointed Doll, 8", manufactured by Schoenhut, copyright Pat Sullivan, 1920s, $450.00 – 700.00.

Scrappy Character Pull Toy, ©Columbia Pictures, 1930s. Extremely rare cartoon character toy, $600.00 – 1,000.00.

Scrappy Big Little Book, ©Columbia Pictures, 1930s, $35.00 – 60.00.

Felix the Cat Rubber Squeak Toy, ©Pat Sullivan, $50.00 – 75.00.

Scrappy Cartoon Character Christmas Tree Lights, with Mazda Lamps. Photo shows lamp and inside box stand-up flap, 1930s, ©Columbia Pictures, $250.00 – 375.00. Exterior of box shown below.

Felix the Cat Target Board, tin litho, manufactured by Lido Toys, $45.00 – 65.00.

Heckle and Jeckle and The Runaway Balloon, child's storybook, 1960s, $10.00 – 20.00.

Betty Boop, Bimbo, and Ko Ko Character Guitar, ©Max Fleischer, 1930s, $200.00 – 350.00.

Early Cartoon Character on Rocking Horse, unmarked but possibly Warner Brothers Sniffles or Krazy Kat Character Mouse. Manufactured by Toy King Toys, 1930s, $125.00 – 250.00.

Popeye the Champ Boxed Tin Wind-up Celluloid Figure, in original box by Marx, ©King Features Syndicate, $2,500.00 – 4,000.00.

Walking Popeye with Parrot Cages Tin Character Wind-up, ©King Features Syndicate, 1930s. Shown with original box, $850.00 – 1,100.00.

Popeye and Olive Oyl "Slinky" Pull Toy by Line Mar, Japan, ©King Features, 1960s, $500.00 – 750.00.

Popeye Cast Iron Lamp with Figural Popeye Light Filament, 1930s. Rare and unusual, $350.00 – 500.00.

Popeye Tin Daily Quarter Bank, ©King Features, $125.00 – 200.00.

Popeye Pilot Tin Wind-up Plane, ©King Features Syndicate, 1930s, $600.00 – 850.00.

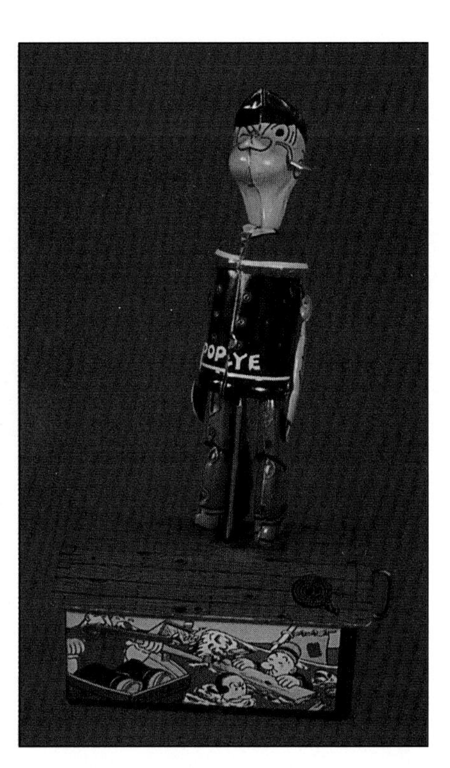

Popeye Single Figure Roof Dancer Tin Wind-up, by J. Chein, 1930s, $750.00 – 1,000.00.

Popeye Bubble Target, beautiful 1930s large tin lithographed example, ©King Features Syndicate, $500.00 – 700.00.

Popeye and Olive Oyl Roof Dancer Tin Litho Wind-up Toy, manufactured by J. Chein, ©King Features, $1,000.00 – 1,500.00.

Bubble Blowing Battery-operated Popeye, in original box, manufactured by Line Mar, ©King Features Syndicate, $800.00 – 1,200.00.

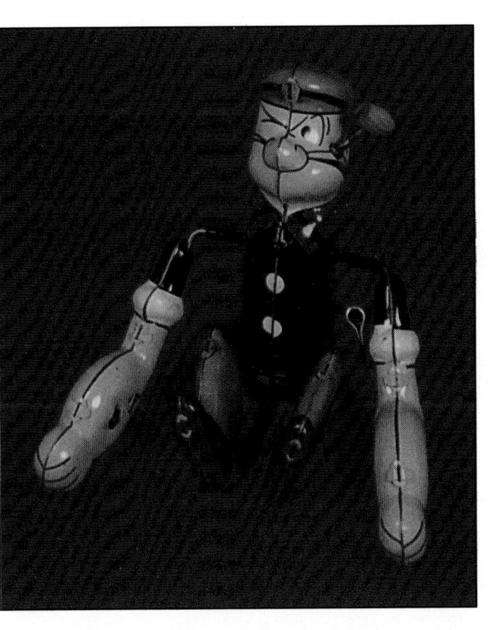

Popeye Tin Wind-up Tumbling Toy by Line Mar, Japan, ©King Features Syndicate. Rare, $1,000.00 – 1,400.00.

Popeye Basketball Shooter Tin Wind-up Toy by Line Mar, Japan, ©King Features, $1,200.00 – 1,800.00.

Popeye Menu Bagatelle Game, ©King Features, 1930s, with superb color lithography, $450.00 – 700.00.

Popeye Paper Litho on Wood Ring Toss Game, ©King Features, 1930s. Rare toy, $500.00 – 750.00.

Popeye Cheers Christmas Lamps, ©King Features Syndicate, 1930s, $150.00 – 225.00.

Popeye, Wimpy, and Olive Oyl Character Soap, ©King Features Syndicate, circa 1930s. In original box, $175.00 – 250.00.

Popeye Tin Wind-up Tank Toy by Line Mar, Japan, ©King Features, $600.00 – 900.00.

Popeye and Bluto Tin and Celluloid Wind-up Boxing Toy by Line Mar, ©King Features, $1,800.00 – 2,500.00.

"Popeye Spinach" Pop-up Can Toy, tin and plastic, ©King Features Syndicate, $75.00 – 125.00.

Popeye Punching Bag Tin Wind-up Toy by J. Chein, ©King Features, 1930s, $1,900.00 – 2,600.00.

Popeye Wood Jointed Composition Doll, with original bag, ©King Features, 1930s. Very rare, $1,200.00 – 1,700.00.

"Musical Popeye The Sailorman" Toy Figure. Approx. 14", in original box, $500.00 – 850.00.

Popeye Ghost Ship to Treasure Island, small paperback book, ©King Features Syndicate, $5.00 – 10.00.

Popeye Metal Brush with Popeye Logo, ©King Features, 1930s, $50.00 – 75.00.

Popeye and Sweet Pea Musical Pull Toy, ©King Features Syndicate, $250.00 – 400.00.

Popeye in the Music Box Jack-In-The-Box, with great colorful litho characters on all sides. Manufactured by Mattel, ©King Features, $125.00 – 200.00.

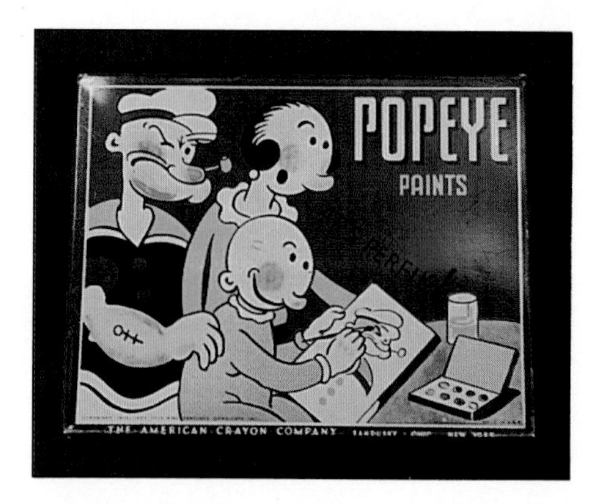

Popeye Paints by The American Crayon Co. of Sandusky Ohio, in original metal box, ©King Features Syndicate, $55.00 – 95.00.

Popeye White Chalk in original box, manufactured by The American Crayon Company of Sandusky, Ohio, King Features Syndicate, 1936, $65.00 – 110.00.

Popeye Chalk Box (reverse) showing colorful Popeye character scene.

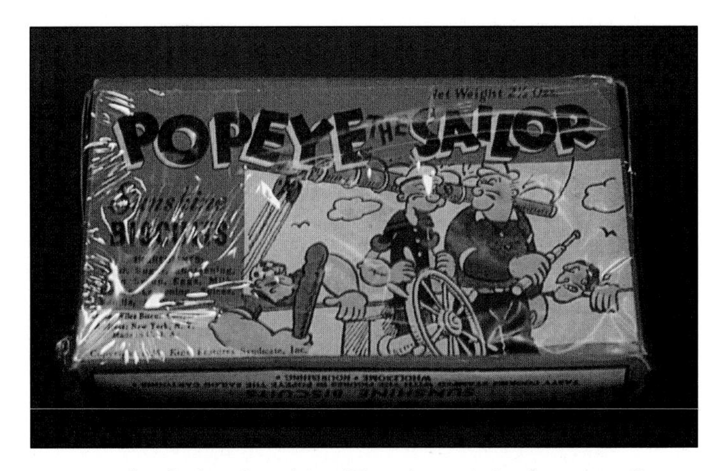

Popeye the Sailor Sunshine Biscuits, original carton, Copyright King Features Syndicate, $150.00 – 250.00.

Popeye Tin Litho Alarm Clock, ©King Features, 1930s, reverse view is below, $850.00 – 1,450.00.

Bluto and Olive Oyl Wooden Paper Litho Pull Toy, circa 1930s, $125.00 – 200.00.

Popeye Wind-up Punching Bag Toy by Chein, 1930s, $750.00 – 1,000.00.

Popeye and Sweet Pea Wooden Paper Litho Pull Toy, circa 1930s, $125.00 – 200.00.

Popeye Celluloid Figure with Pipe, made in Japan, 1930s, $275.00 – 500.00.

Popeye Soft Rubber Night Light. Entire figure lights up from inside, $125.00 – 200.00.

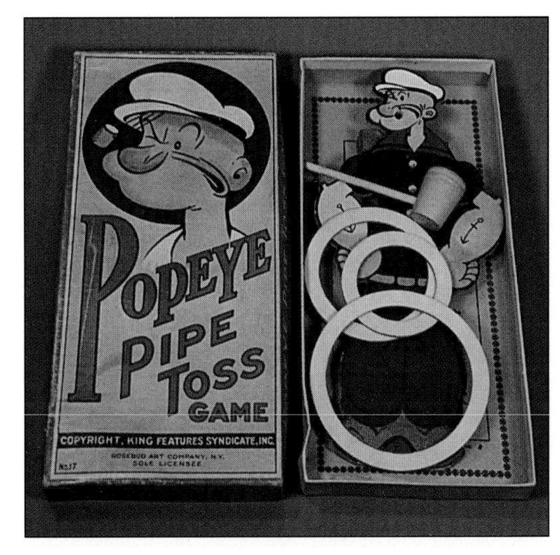

Popeye Pipe Toss Game, manufactured by Rosebud Art Company of New York, copyright King Features Syndicate, 1930s. Game shown is complete (pipe and rings are often missing), $75.00 – 150.00.

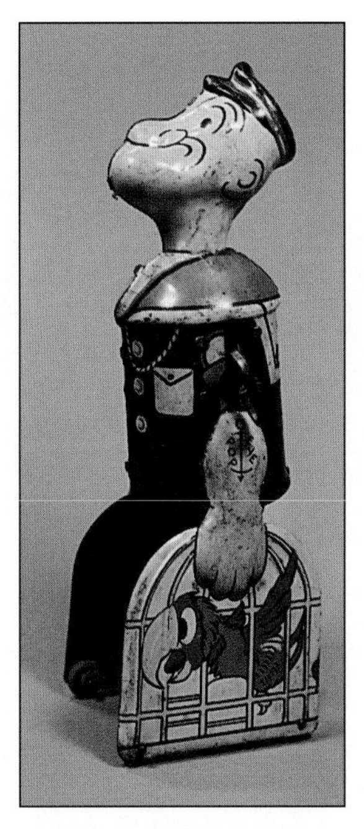

Popeye Tin Wind-up, Express Toy featuring Popeye carrying twin parrot cages, ©King Features, 1930s, $400.00 – 700.00.

Barnacle Bill Wind-up Toy, based on Popeye character design by J. Chein, 1930s, $450.00 – 800.00.

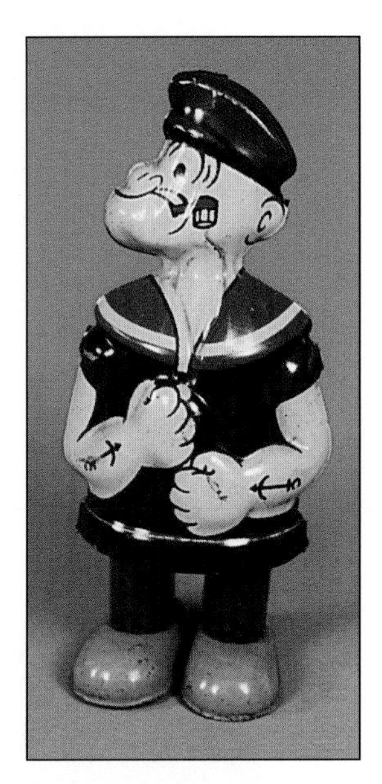

Popeye Wind-up Walker by J. Chein and ©King Features Syndicate, 1930s, $700.00 – 900.00.

Walking Popeye with Parrot Cages, tin wind-up with original box, 1930s, $850.00 – 1,100.00.

Popeye Express Tin Wind-up Character Toy, ©King Features, 1930s, $600.00 – 950.00.

Popeye Lantern by Line Mar, Japan, ©King Features, shown with original box, $400.00 – 650.00.

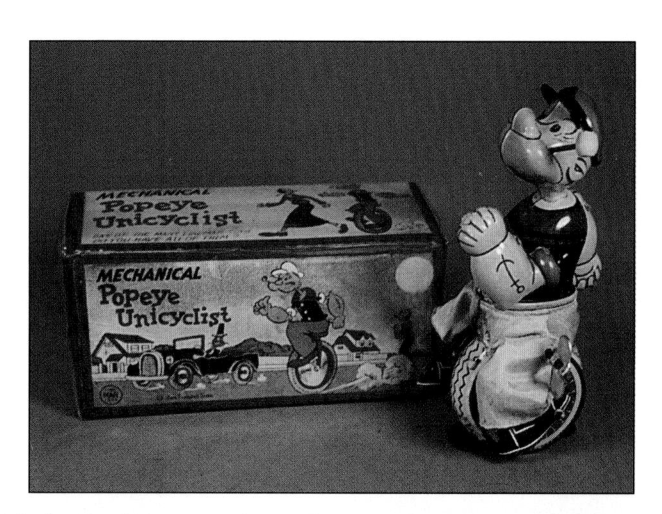

Mechanical Popeye Unicyclist Wind-up Toy, with original box, manufactured by Line Mar, Japan, ©King Features Syndicate, $900.00 – 1,200.00.

Popeye's Colored Chalk, manufactured by The American Crayon Company of Sandusky, Ohio, ©King Features Syndicate, $75.00 – 125.00.

Reverse colorful box art of Popeye Colored Chalk.

Popeye "Barnacle Bill," look-alike knock-off character in barrel wind-up, manufactured by J. Chein, $450.00 – 700.00.

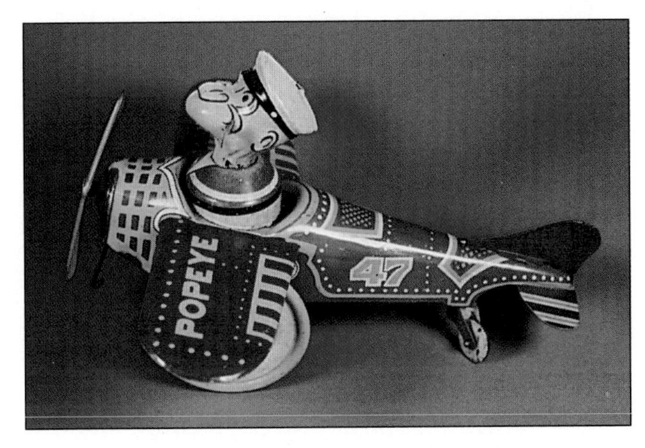

Popeye Pilot Tin Wind-up Airplane Toy by J. Chein, ©King Features Syndicate, 1930s. Early, rare version of Popeye Pilot, $900.00 – 1,200.00.

Popeye Character Celluloid Figure Tin Wind-up Dippy Dumper Toy, 1930s, $800.00 – 1,200.00.

Popeye Express Tin Wind-up Flying Planes Toy, manufactured by Marx, King Features, 1930s. Rare complete with Planes, $1,200.00 – 1,800.00.

Bluto, Popeye Character Celluloid Figure Dippy Dumper Tin Wind-up, 1930s, $800.00 – 1,200.00.

Popeye the Sailor Pencil Box, manufactured by Dixon, King Features Syndicate, 1934. Reverse shown below, $75.00 – 125.00.

Popeye Cast Iron Delivery Cart with Popeye Figure inside, 1930s, $700.00 – 900.00.

Popeye Transit Co. Friction Metal Truck by Line Mar, ©King Features, $750.00 – 950.00.

Popeye Mechanical Roller Skater by Line Mar, ©King Features. With original box, $1,000 – 1,500.00.

Popeye Wood Jointed Composition Doll, ©King Features, 1930s, $750.00 – 1,000.00.

Popeye Cast Iron Doorstop, original finish, 1930s. Rarely found with bright paint in original condition, $1,500.00 – 2,500.00.

Woody Woodpecker, Walter Lantz Character Film by Castle Films, in original box, $20.00 – 35.00.

Popeye Cloth and Plastic Character Doll, probably 1950s or earlier, $200.00 – 400.00.

Ignatz Mouse Early Cartoon Character Tricycle, rare wood and metal toy, 1930s. Often mistaken for Mickey Mouse, but not a Disney character, $950.00 – 1,400.00.

Woody Woodpecker Cookie Jar, ©Walter Lantz, recent. An excellent likeness of the character, $700.00 – 900.00.

Woody Woodpecker Talking Puppet by Mattel, ©Walter Lantz, 1960s, $45.00 – 70.00.

Woody Woodpecker Storybook published by Whitman, ©Walter Lantz, $15.00 – 20.00.

Woody Woodpecker Mattel Music Maker, manufactured by Mattel, ©Walter Lantz, 1960s. Plays Woody Woodpecker theme song, $40.00 – 65.00.

Woody Woodpecker Hard Plastic Character Clock with Action Pendulum, ©Walter Lantz, circa 1950s, $275.00 – 425.00.

Walter Lantz's Woody Woodpecker and The Meteor Menace Comic Storybook, $6.00 – 12.00.

Dick Tracy's Bonny Braids Doll, with original box, 1950s, $250.00 – 400.00.

Dick Tracy Detective Set by J. Pressman and C. Chester Gould, circa 1940. Unusual boxed playset, $125.00 – 200.00.

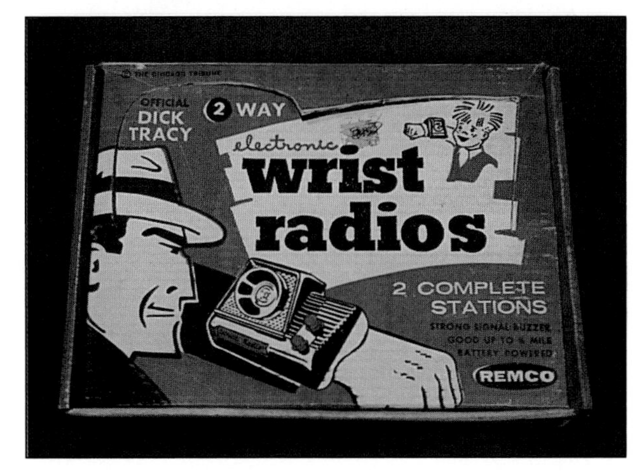

Dick Tracy 2-way Electronic Wrist Radios by Remco, ©The Chicago Tribune, 1960s, $95.00 – 150.00.

Superman Ceramic Telephone Booth Cookie Jar, recent. Unusual style and highly desirable because of current cookie jar market, $700.00 – 950.00.

Dick Tracy Squad Car No.1, tin toy car by Louis Marx, $200.00 – 325.00.

Dick Tracy Metal Siren Pistol, featuring siren sound of gun when trigger is pulled, $150.00 – 225.00.

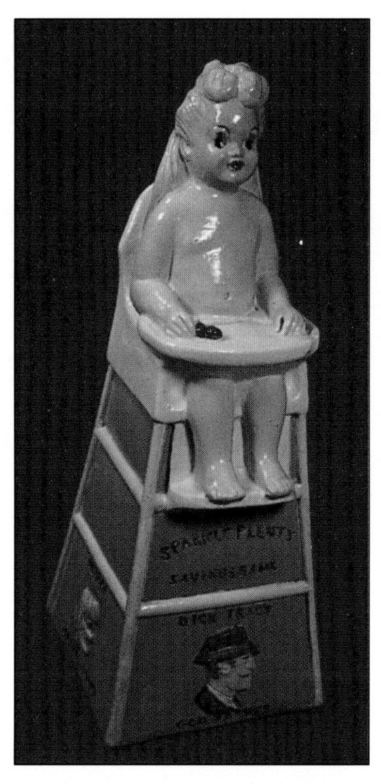

Dick Tracy Sparkle Plenty Savings Bank, plaster composition bank showing Baby Sparkle in a high chair, $600.00 – 850.00.

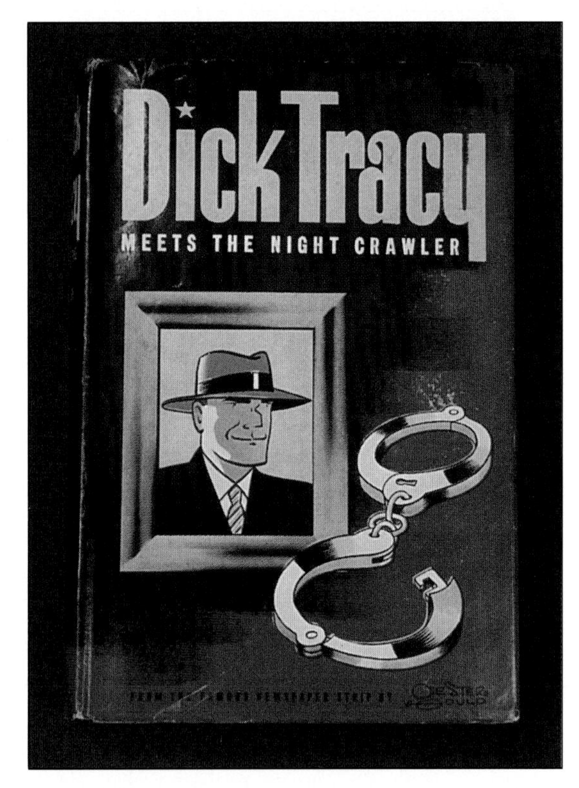

Dick Tracy Meets the Night Crawler, book with original dust jacket, ©Chester Gould, $20.00 – 35.00.

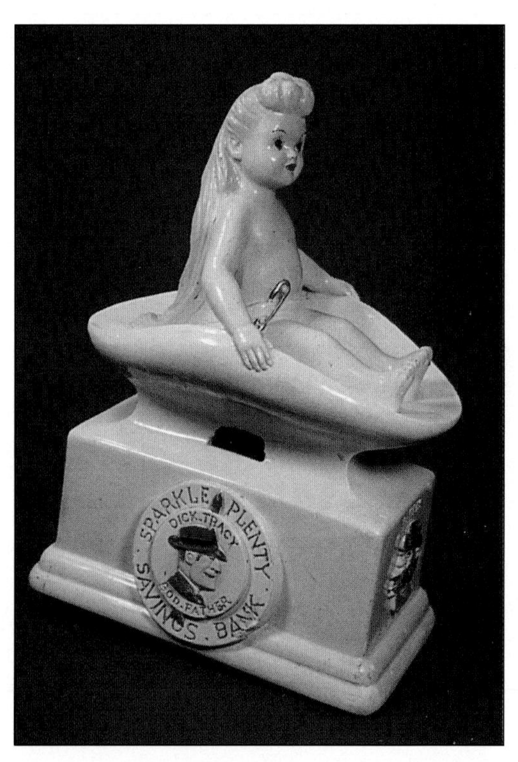

Dick Tracy Sparkle Plenty Baby Scale Design Plaster Composition Savings Bank. Rarely found in such superb condition, $700.00 – 1,000.00.

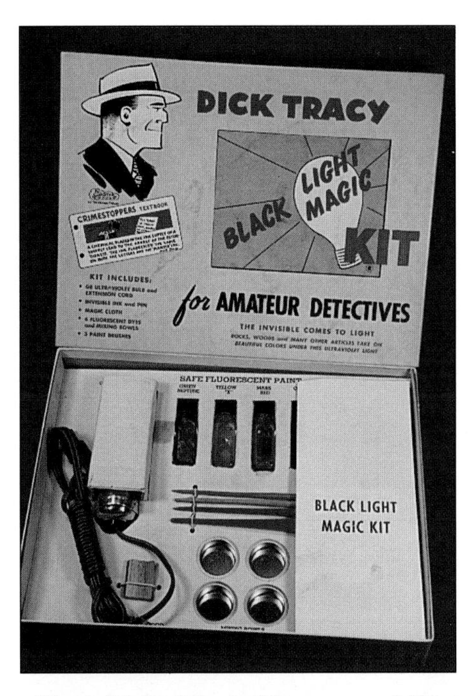

Dick Tracy Black Light Magic Kit, unusual "Detective Set for Amateur Detectives," ©Chester Gould, $125.00 – 200.00.

Mr. Magoo Character Battery-operated Metal Toy Car, circa 1960s, $275.00 – 450.00.

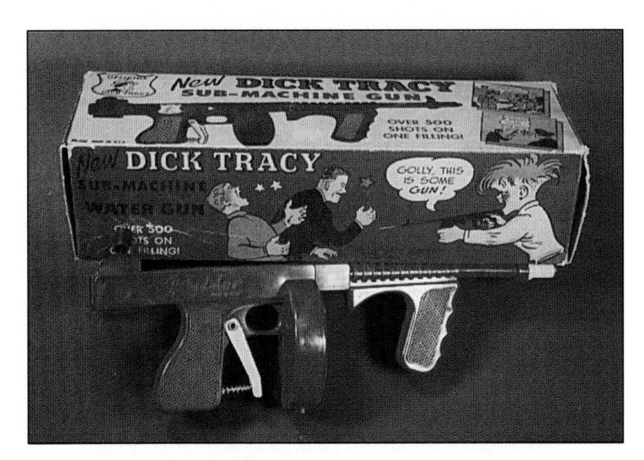

Dick Tracy Sub-Machine Water Gun, with original box, 1950s, $150.00 – 225.00.

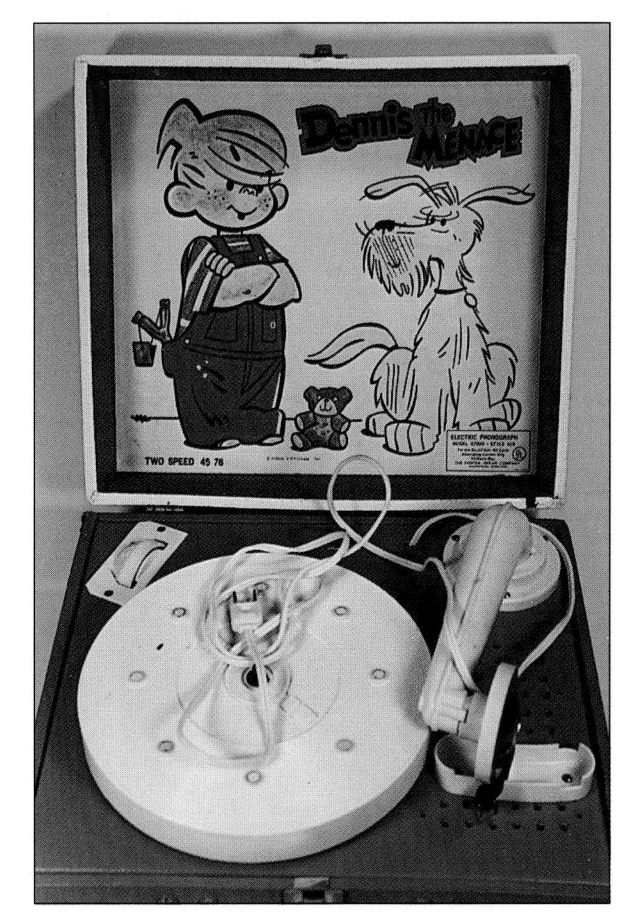

Dennis the Menace Portable Phonograph, © Hank Ketcham, 1960s, $75.00 – 150.00.

Sparkle Plenty Christmas Tree Lights with Character Decorated Lamps, colorful box, $150.00 – 250.00.

Tom and Jerry Musical Guitar by Mattel Toys, by ©MGM, 1960s. Striking die-cut molded character design, $125.00 – 175.00.

Carl Laemmle presents Oswald the Lucky Rabbit, The Big Little Book, 1930s, $40.00 – 65.00.

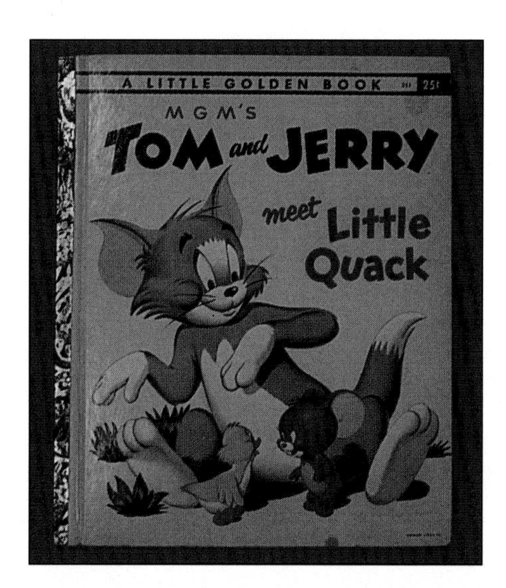

MGM's Tom and Jerry Meet Little Quack, Whitman Little Golden Book, $15.00 – 20.00.

Tom and Jerry "Tom" Talking Hand Puppet by Mattel Toys, ©MGM, circa 1960, $50.00 – 70.00.

MGM's Tom and Jerry Merry Christmas Little Golden Book, $15.00 – 20.00.

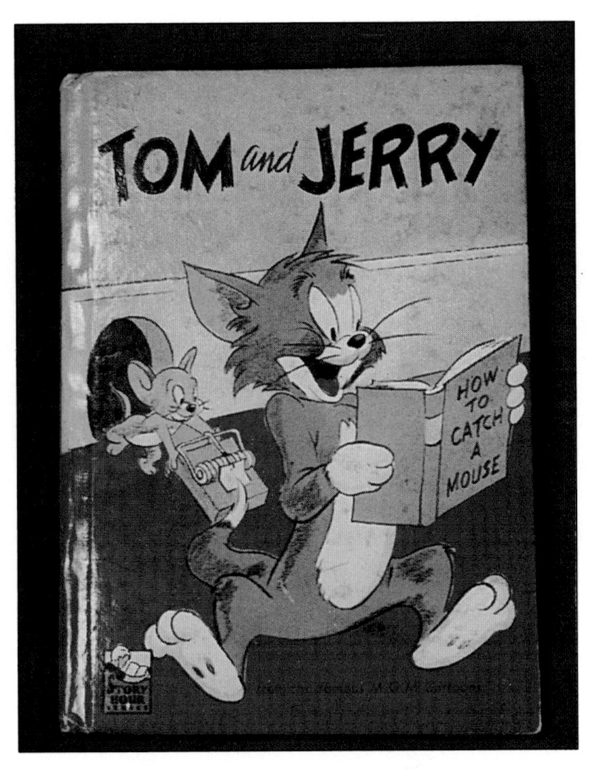

Tom and Jerry Storybook from the MGM Cartoons by Story Hour Books, $18.00 – 30.00.

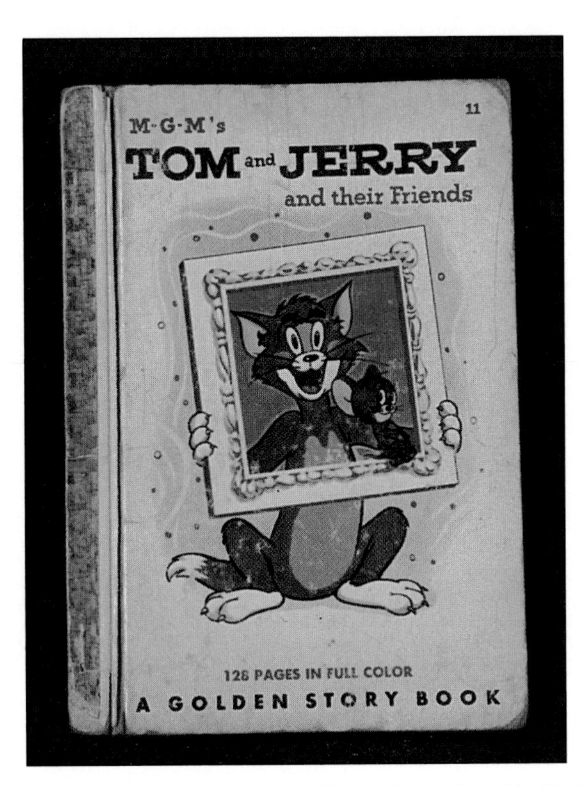

MGM's Tom and Jerry and Their Friends, "A Golden Storybook," 1950s, $15.00 – 25.00.

Tom and Jerry Mattel Music Maker, manufactured by Mattel, ©MGM, 1960s, reverse shown below, $50.00 – 75.00.

"Tom and Jerry Meet Mr. Fingers," children's book, ©MGM, circa 1950s, $10.00 – 15.00.

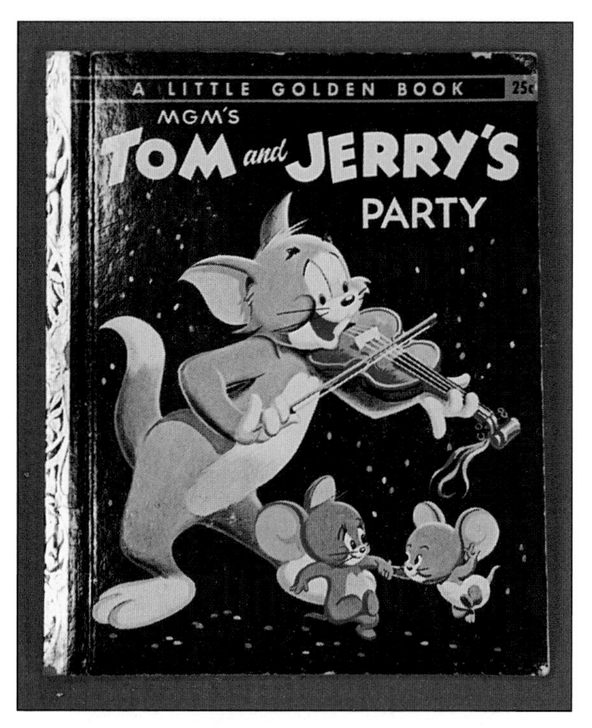

"MGM's Tom and Jerry's Party," a Little Golden Book featuring the popular MGM characters, $12.00 – 18.00.

Beany-Cecil and Their Pals Child's Record Player, ©Bob Clampett, 1960s. Rare, $250.00 – 400.00.

Beany Character Doll, ©Bob Clampett, circa 1960, $125.00 – 200.00.

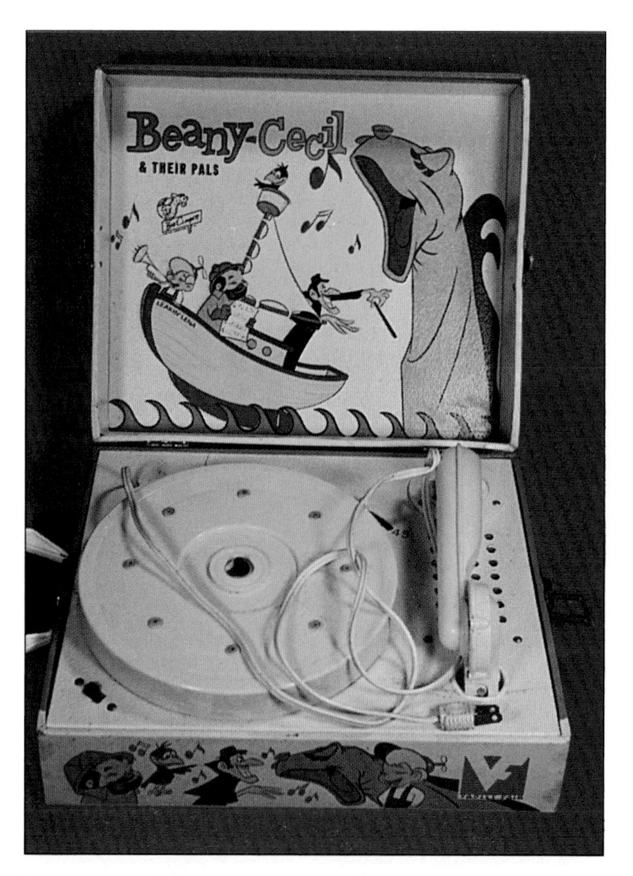

Inside detail of Beany and Cecil Record Player pictured above.

Beany and Cecil Cartoon Kit, early Colorforms Toy, ©Bob Clampett, 1960s, $80.00 – 125.00.

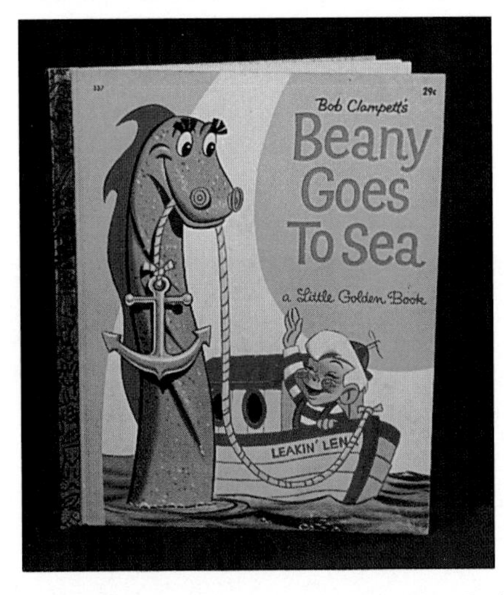

Bob Clampett's Beany Goes To Sea Little Golden Book, ©Bob Clampett, circa 1959, $15.00 – 25.00.

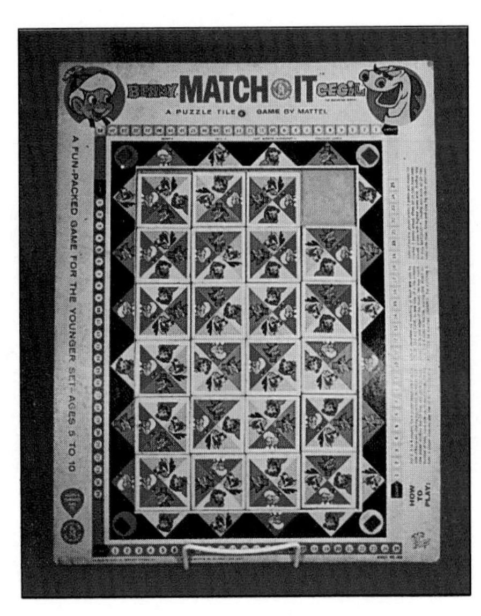

Mattel Puzzle Tile Beany and Cecil "Match It" Game, ©Bob Clampett, early 1960s, $75.00 – 90.00.

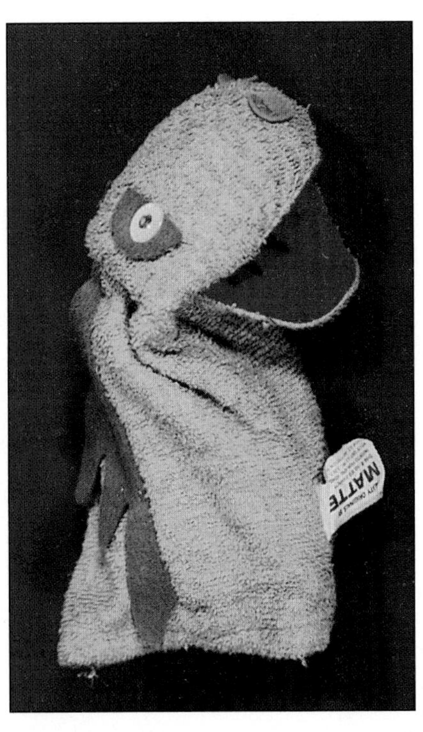

Cecil Hand Puppet by Mattel Toys, 1960s. Constructed mainly of terry cloth, $50.00 – 75.00.

Cecil Plastic Character Figure Bank, $30.00 – 45.00.

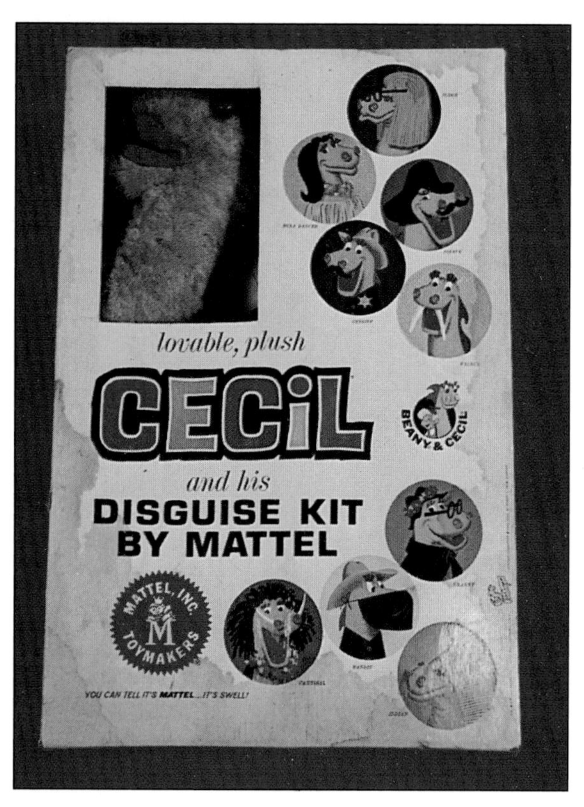

Cecil and His Disguise Kit by Mattel, from The Beany and Cecil Cartoon Series, circa 1960. Featuring wonderful box cover and clever disguises, $135.00 – 200.00.

Cecil Character Talking Plush Toy by Mattel, 1960s, $125.00 – 200.00.

Bart Simpson PVC Figural Toys, recent, $3.00 – 6.00 each.

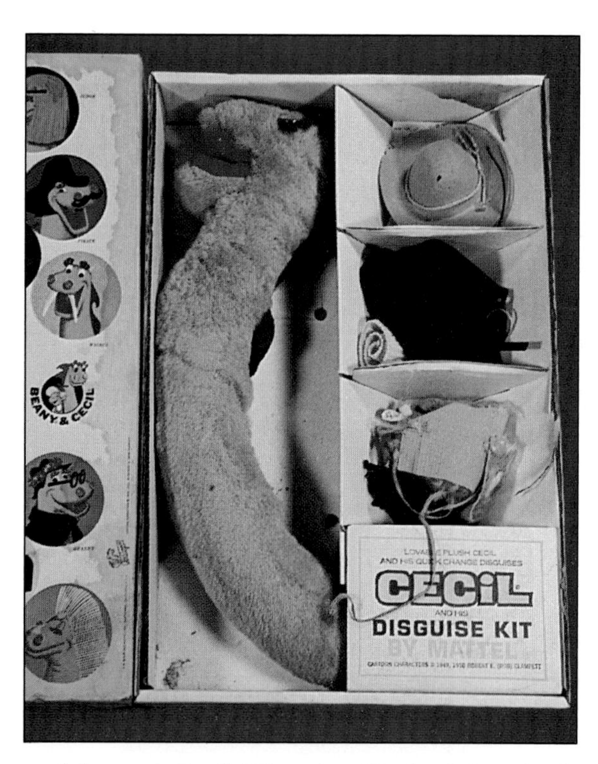

Opened box of Cecil Disguise Kit by Mattel, shown above.

Snoopy Space Patrol Battery-operated Spaceship Toy, Japan, ©Charles M. Schulz, 1960s, $350.00 – 600.00.

Snoopy Dressed in Tuxedo and Top Hat Push Puppet Plastic Character Toy, ©Charles M. Schulz, $50.00 – 75.00.

Snoopy Bathtub Soap Toy Figure, ©Charles M. Schulz, $20.00 – 30.00.

Snoopy Bubble Bath Container, ©Charles M. Schulz, $15.00 – 25.00.

Snoopy Painted Ceramic Character and Doghouse Figure, ©Charles M. Schulz, $25.00 – 40.00.

Snoopy Glazed Composition Figure/Paperweight with caption "I'm allergic to morning." ©Charles M. Schulz, $20.00 – 35.00.

Peanuts Lunch Box by Thermos, ©Charles M. Schulz. Featuring comic strip illustrations, $50.00 – 75.00.

Snoopy Character Valentine's Collectors Plate, ©Charles M. Schulz, 1979, $20.00 – 35.00.

Lucy and Linus Peanuts Character Dolls by Charles Schulz, 1960s, $45.00 – 70.00 each.

Peanuts Character Toys by Charles M. Schulz, 1960s, $35.00 – 65.00 each.

Snoopy Sno-Cones Ice Treat Maker featuring Lucy and Charlie Brown, recent, $35.00 – 65.00.

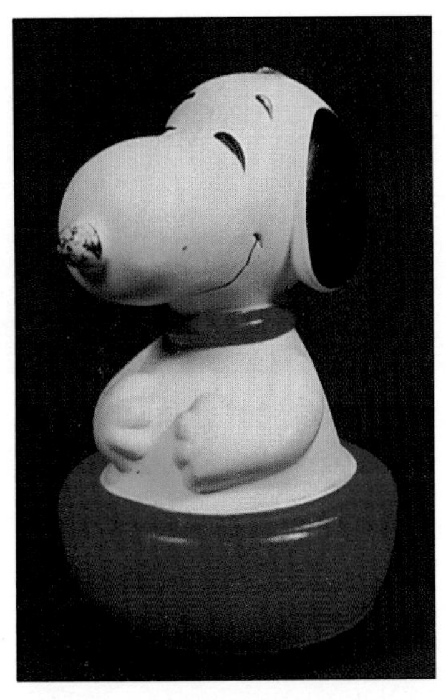

Snoopy Vinyl Roly-Poly Bathtub Infant's Toy, ©Charles M. Schulz, $20.00 – 40.00.

Snoopy Die Cast Metal Toy in original box, manufactured by Aviva, ©Charles Schulz, 1970s. Charlie Brown drives while Snoopy, Lucy, and Woodstock ride along, $65.00 – 85.00.

Peanuts Character Lunch Box, featuring Snoopy as a Scout and Woodstock, ©Charles M. Schulz, $65.00 – 95.00.

Linus Vinyl Toy, ©Charles Schulz, Peanuts, 1960s, $25.00 – 45.00.

Snoopy Character Vinyl Doll Dressed as Santa, ©Charles M. Schulz, $20.00 – 35.00.

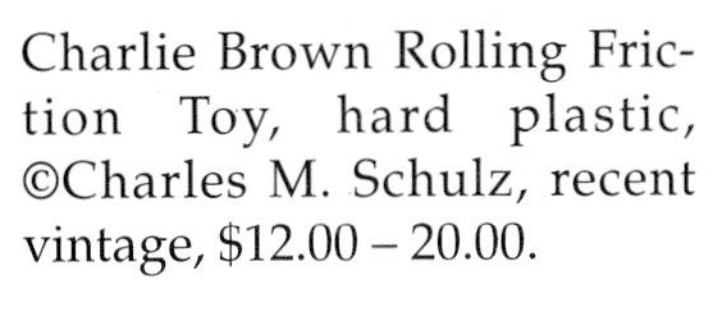

Charlie Brown Rolling Friction Toy, hard plastic, ©Charles M. Schulz, recent vintage, $12.00 – 20.00.

"Here Comes Snoopy Book" published by Fawcett Crest, ©Charles M. Schulz, 1960s, $5.00 – 10.00.

Charlie Brown Riding a Skateboard, PVC figure, ©United Features Syndicate and Charles M. Schulz, recent, $8.00 – 12.00.

Snoopy and Woodstock on a Skateboard Plastic Toy, ©Charles M. Schulz, recent, $8.00 – 12.00.

Peanuts Characters 1960s Bus (with sound), ©Charles M. Schulz, United Features Syndicate, $200.00 – 350.00.

Snoopy Astronaut Character Figure, ©Charles M. Schulz, 1960s, $100.00 – 150.00.

Snoopy in the Music Box by Mattel, ©United Features Syndicate and Charles M. Schulz, 1960s, $60.00 – 95.00.

Snoopy Die-Cast "Red Baron" Bi-Plane by Aviva, ©United Features Syndicate and Charles M. Schulz, 1970s, $25.00 – 45.00.

Lucy Cloth Doll, Charles M. Schulz, 1960s, $30.00 – 40.00.

Linus Vinyl Character Toy, ©Charles M. Schulz and United Features Syndicate, $15.00 – 25.00.

Snoopy Plastic Friction Delivery Truck, ©United Features Syndicate and Charles M. Schulz, recent, $15.00 – 25.00.

Snoopy Character Plastic Rolling Toy, ©Charles M. Schulz, 1960s or newer. Rolls like a yo-yo, Snoopy stays upright, $12.00 – 20.00.

Peanuts Jigsaw Puzzle, ©Charles M. Schulz, 1960s, $45.00 – 75.00.

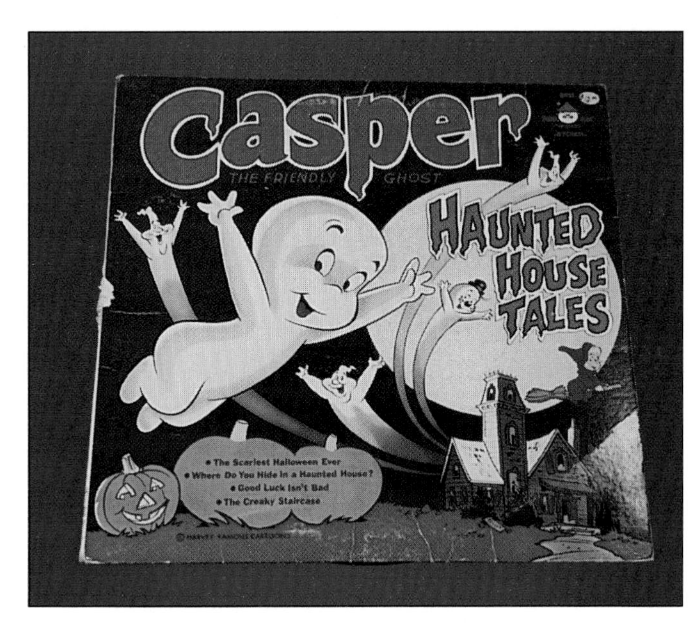

Casper Haunted House Tales, ©Harvey Cartoons, 1960s, $25.00 – 50.00.

Charlie Brown Character Mug, ©Charles M. Schulz, recent, $10.00 – 20.00.

Casper the Friendly Ghost Vinyl Character Doll, ©Harvey Cartoons. An excellent likeness of the character, $15.00 – 30.00.

Casper the Friendly Ghost Game by Milton Bradley, ©Harvey Cartoons, 1960s, $35.00 – 55.00.

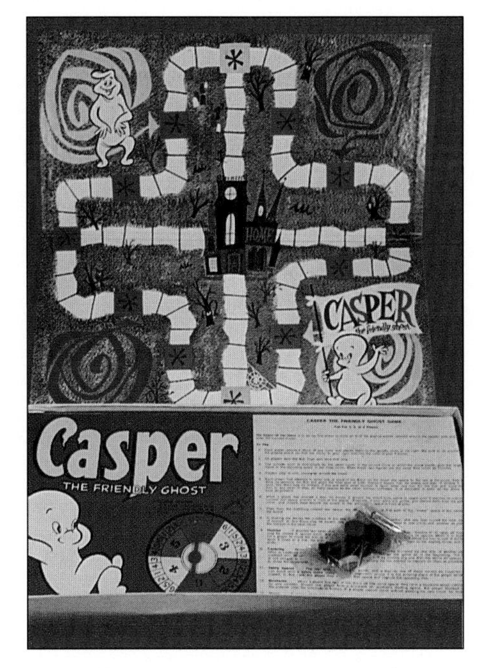

Game Board, Tokens, Spinner, and Box insert for Casper Game pictured above.

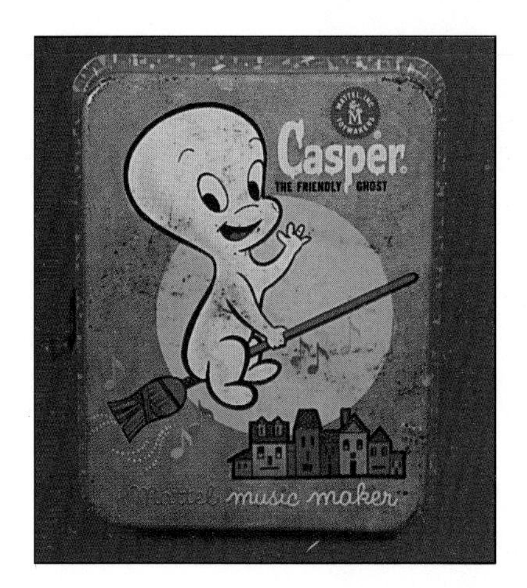

Casper the Friendly Ghost Mattel Music Maker Tin Wind-up Crank Music Box by Mattel Toys, Inc., ©Harvey Comics, Inc., 1960s, $45.00 – 70.00.

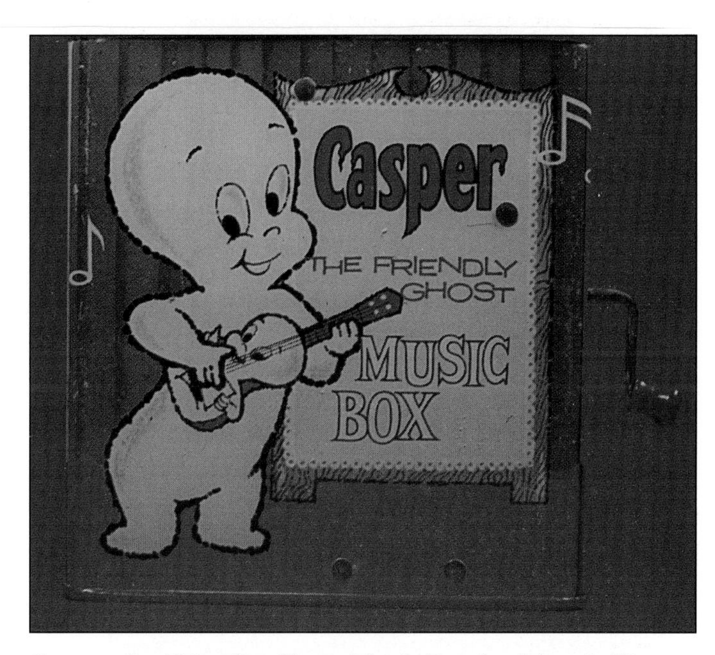

Casper the Friendly Ghost Music Box by Mattel, Harvey Cartoons, 1960. Plays Casper theme song, $45.00 – 65.00.

Casper the Friendly Ghost Jack-in-the-Box, $45.00 – 65.00.

Casper the Friendly Ghost and Little Audrey Record by Little Golden Records, ©Harvey Comics, 1960s, $20.00 – 35.00.

Batmobile, Batman and Robin Vehicle, 1960s or later with Batman Logo on wheels and complete with two dolls, $90.00 – 140.00.

Batman and Robin Bookends, plaster composition, circa 1960s, $150.00 – 225.00 pair.

Batman Talking Alarm Clock, with original box, 1960s or later, $85.00 – 135.00.

Batman Glazed Ceramic Bank, 1960s, $100.00 – 150.00.

Batman Battery-operated Toothbrush, with interchangeable brush, recent, $10.00 – 20.00.

Batman Batcycle Vehicle Toy, with logo sticker, 1960s or later, $75.00 – 120.00.

Captain America Mechanical Super Hero Tricycle by Line Mar, ©Marvel Comics, 1960s. Rare comic character figure, $400.00 – 650.00.

Marvel Super Heroes Role Playing Game by TSR, ©Marvel Comics, recent, $20.00 – 35.00.

The Amazing Spider-Man Fantastic Four Game by Milton Bradley, recent, $25.00 – 35.00.

"The Amazing Spider-Man" Game Board for boxed game, colorful display board. ©Marvel Comics, $25.00 – 35.00.

Amazing Spider-Man Toy, ©Marvel Comics, "Supersize Super Heroes," recent toy in beautiful display box, $15.00 – 25.00.

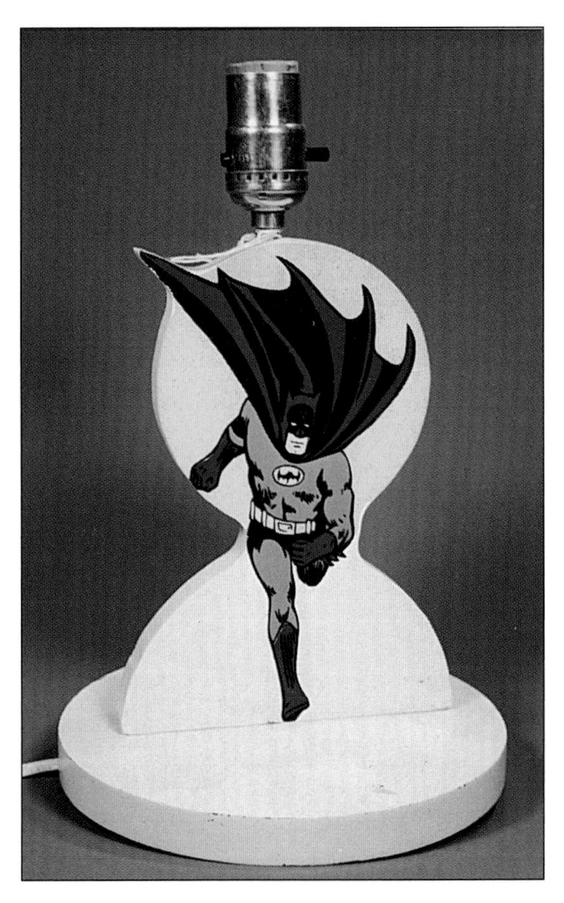

Batman Character Lamp, wood construction, circa 1970s, $50.00 – 75.00.

Wonder Woman Girl's Blue Lunch Kit or Carrying Case, ©DC Comics, 1977, $20.00 – 30.00.

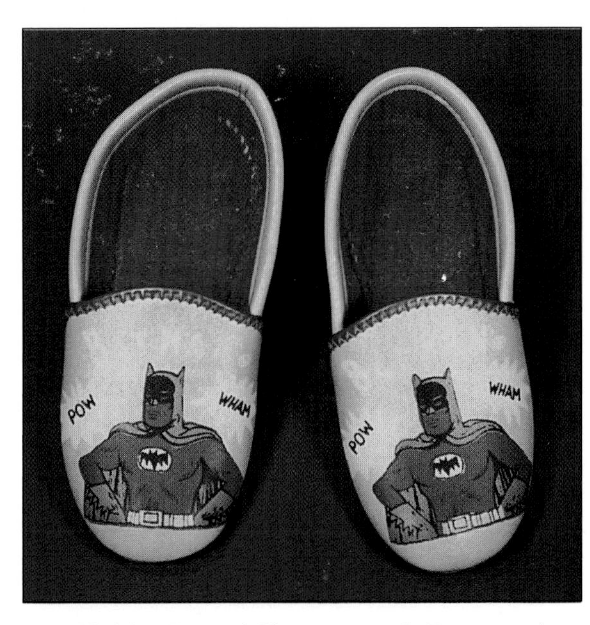

Batman Child's Pair of Slippers with Batman character logo, 1960s, $35.00 – 60.00.

Smurf Plastic Character Bank, ©Peyo, circa 1980s, $20.00 – 40.00.

Smurf Character Plastic Bank, circa 1980s, $25.00 – 40.00.

Smurf PVC Plastic Characters, ©Peyo, 1970s–1980s, $5.00 – 15.00 each.

Smurf Character PVC Toys, ©Peyo, recent, $5.00 – 15.00 each.

Mr. Magoo Soaky Toy, manufactured by Colgate, 1960s, $15.00 – 30.00.

Alvin the Chipmunk Vinyl Character Bank, recent, $20.00 – 30.00.

Alvin Character Soaky Toy by Colgate-Palmolive, 1960s, $20.00 – 35.00.

Alvin, Simon, and Theodore Chipmunks Characters, recent PVC figures, $3.00 – 5.00 each.

Alvin the Chipmunk Soaky Toy, 1960s, $15.00 – 30.00.

Alvin and Theodore PVC Characters, recent, $3.00 – 5.00 each.

Smurfs Character PVC Figures, ©Peyo, 1980s, $6.00 – 12.00 each.

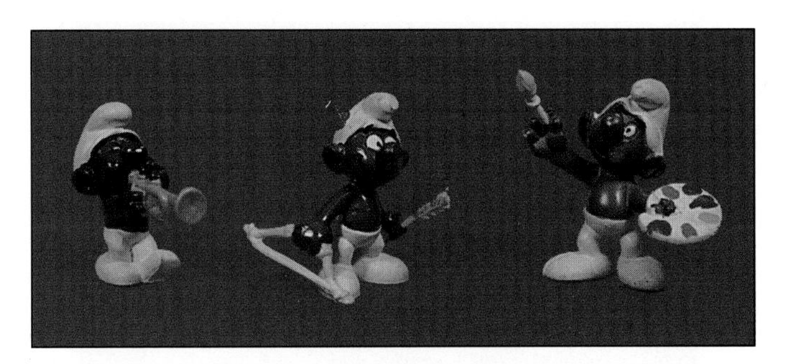

Smurfs Character PVC Figures, 1980s, $6.00 – 12.00.

Smurfs Character PVC Figures, 1980s, $6.00 – 12.00.

Smurfs Character Figures, ©Peyo, $7.00 – 15.00.

Smurfs Plastic Character Cup, ©Peyo, 1980s, $10.00 – 15.00.

Super Smurf Student Notebook, ©Peyo, 1980s, $7.00 – 12.00.

The Astrosmurf–A Smurf Adventure by Peyo, published by Random House, recent, $10.00 – 15.00.

Mattel Preschool Magic Talk Papa Smurf's Lab, ©Peyo, recent, $35.00 – 50.00.

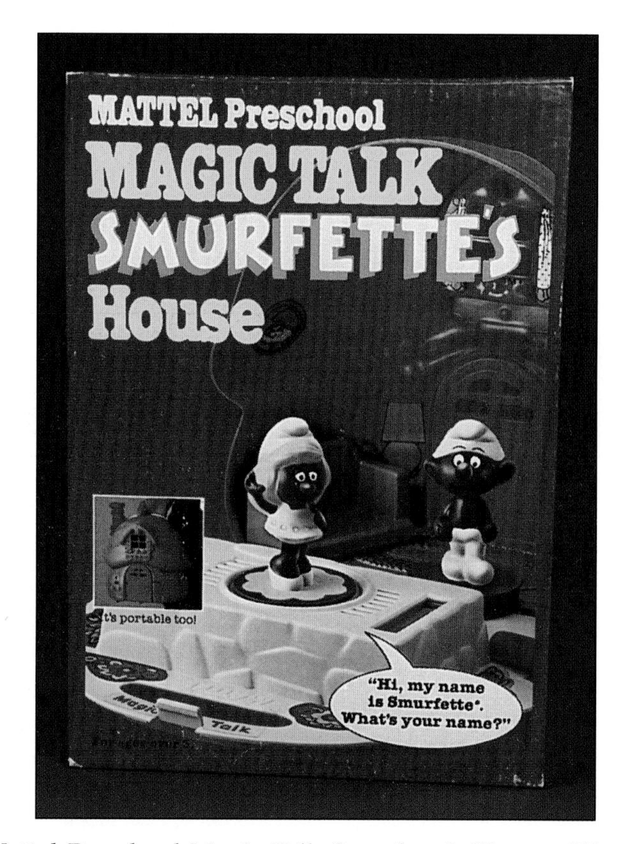

Mattel Preschool Magic Talk Smurfette's House, ©Peyo, recent, $35.00 – 50.00.

Garfield Colorforms Play Set by Jim Davis, 1980s, $20.00 – 35.00.

Garfield Stuffed Plush Character Doll, ©Jim Davis, recent. Common example, $15.00 – 30.00.

Garfield "World's Greatest" Ceramic Figure, ©Jim Davis, circa 1970s, $10.00 – 20.00.

Garfield Character Stuffed Cloth Toy, ©Jim Davis, recent. Showing Garfield wearing his lasagna bib, $35.00 – 50.00.

Garfield Duffle Bag, ©Jim Davis, recent, $15.00 – 25.00.

Felix the Cat Tin Sand Pails, very recent. These new designs are sometimes being passed off as old, but they are new litho designs, $10.00 – 20.00.

Ninja Turtle Figures, ©Mirage Studios, recent, $7.00 – 10.00.

Teenage Mutant Ninja Turtles "Tote Pack,"©Mirage Studios, recent. Featuring cards and stickers set, $10.00 – 15.00.

Teenage Mutant Ninja Turtles Pop-up Storybook, ©Random House, recent, $10.00 – 15.00.

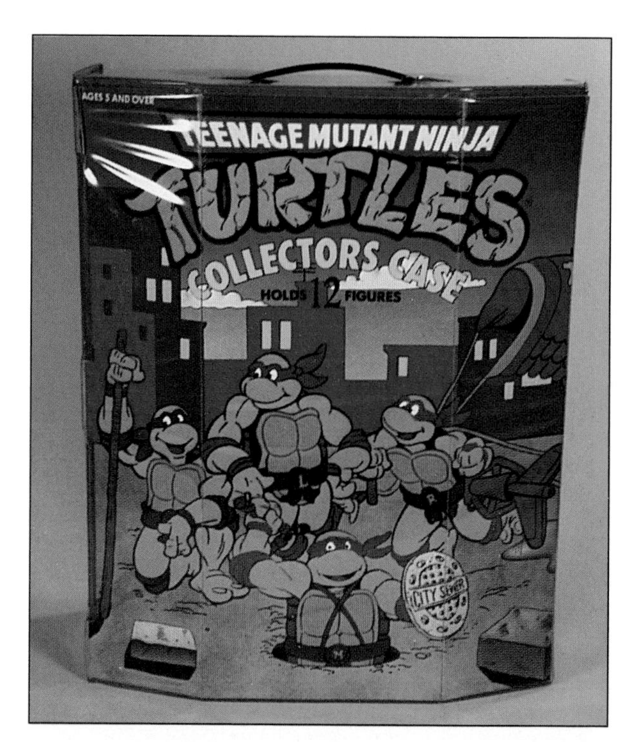

Teenage Mutant Ninja Turtles Collectors Case, ©Mirage Studios, recent. Features wonderful character design on front, $25.00 – 35.00.

Universal Studios Bride of Frankenstein Ninja Turtles Character Figure, ©Mirage, recent, $10.00 – 15.00.

Ninja Turtle Buckles and Novelties, ©Mirage, recent, $5.00 – 10.00 each.

Ninja Turtles Plastic Figures, ©Mirage Studios, recent, $7.00 – 10.00 each.

Ninja Turtle Character Cartoon Dinosaurs, recent, $8.00 – 12.00 each.

Ninja Turtle Character Dinosaur Figure, recent, $8.00 – 12.00.

Teenage Mutant Ninja Turtle Character, Western Character Designs, ©Mirage, recent, $5.00 – 10.00 each.

Teenage Mutant Ninja Turtles Thermos Lunch Bag, ©Mirage, recent, $15.00 – 20.00.

Ninja Turtle Soldier/Cavalry Characters, ©Mirage Studios, recent, $5.00 – 10.00 each.

Ninja Turtle Figure Mini-Play Sets, recent. Head opens to reveal Play Sets inside, $10.00 – 15.00 each.

Teenage Mutant Ninja Turtles Game, ©Mirage Studios and Random House, recent, $15.00 – 25.00.

Ninja Turtle Plastic Soap Holder and Tub Toy, ©Mirage, recent, $5.00 – 10.00.

Ninja Turtle Character Figures, ©Mirage Studios, recent, $5.00 – 10.00 each.

Ninja Turtle "Splinter" Rat Character Figures, ©Mirage Studios, recent, $5.00 – 12.00 each.

Teenage Mutant Ninja Turtles "Olympian" Figures, manufactured by Playmates, ©Mirage Studios, recent, $7.00 – 12.00 each.

Teenage Mutant Ninja Turtles as Troll Figures, ©Mirage Studios, recent, $10.00 – 15.00 each.

Ninja Turtles Space and Military Action Figures, by Playmates Toys, ©Mirage Studios, recent, $5.00 – 10.00 each.

Teenage Mutant Ninja Turtles Star Trek Series Action Figures, ©Mirage and Paramount Studios, recent, $10.00 – 15.00 each.

Ninja Turtle Action figures in "Rap" Outfits, ©Mirage, recent, $5.00 – 10.00 each.

Ninja Turtle Female Character Action Figures including three different versions of April, ©Mirage, recent, $5.00 – 10.00 each.

Ninja Turtle Action Figures, ©Mirage Studios, recent, $5.00 – 10.00 each.

Ninja Turtle Flying Teradactyl Figure by Playmates, ©Mirage, recent, $15.00 – 20.00.

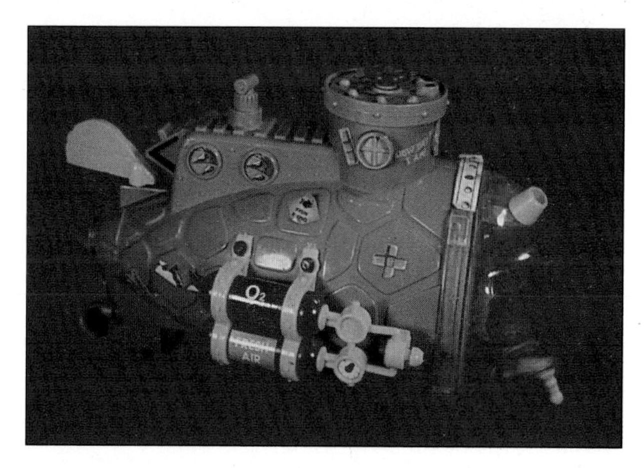

Ninja Turtle Submarine Toy, ©Mirage Studios, recent, $20.00 – 30.00.

Ninja Turtle Monster Figures, ©Mirage Studios, recent, $5.00 – 10.00 each.

Ninja Turtles Newscaster Characters, ©Mirage Studios, recent, $5.00 – 10.00 each.

Ninja Turtle Character Villains, ©Mirage Studios, recent, $5.00 – 10.00 each.

Ninja Turtles Gorilla and Vehicle, ©Mirage, recent, $25.00 – 35.00.

News Channel 6 Ninja Turtle News Team Set, ©Mirage, recent, $50.00 – 75.00.

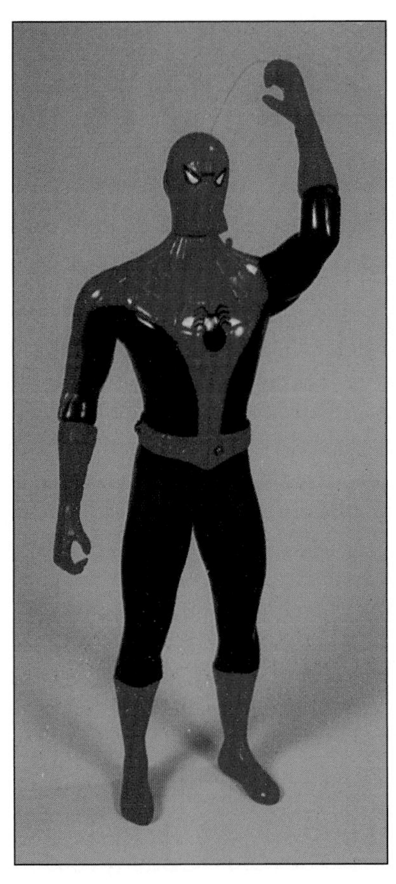

Spider-Man Character Doll, ©Marvel, recent, $15.00 – 25.00.

Bart Simpson Giant Character Plastic Figure, recent, $10.00 – 20.00.

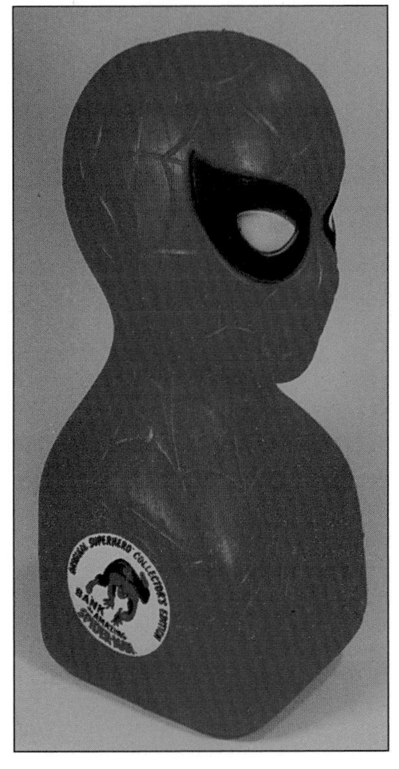

Amazing Spider-Man Collector's Edition Bank, ©Marvel, recent, $25.00 – 35.00.

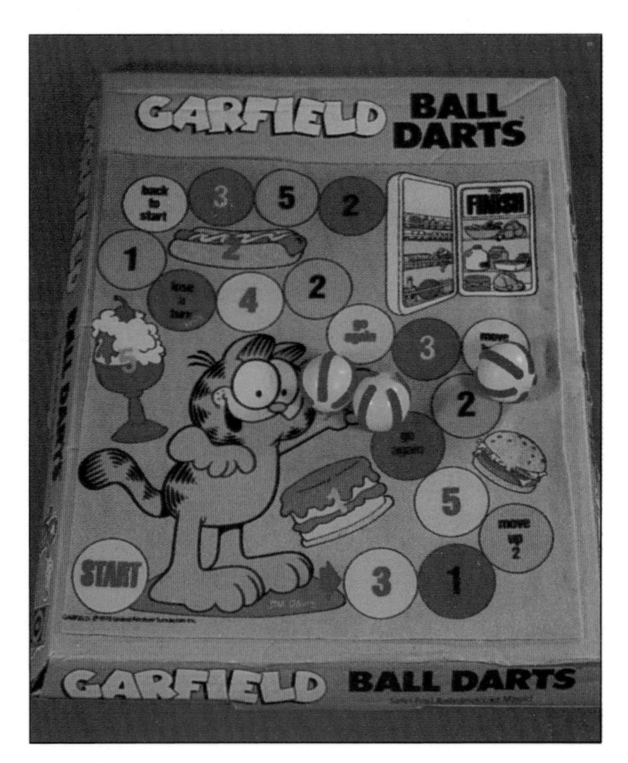

Garfield Ball Darts, ©Jim Davis, recent, $20.00 – 35.00.

ABOUT THE AUTHOR

David Longest is one of Collector Books' most prolific writers with this volume, *Cartoon Toys & Collectibles*, being his sixth book on collecting toys. His first two books, *Character Toys & Collectibles, Series One and Series Two*, were published in the mid-1980s and were soon followed by his large paperback price guide *Toys, Antique & Collectible*. In the early 1990s, he collaborated with Collector Books' Disneyana authority, Michael Stern, to produce his fourth book, *The Collector's Encyclopedia of Disneyana*. In 1994, his book *Antique & Collectible Toys 1870–1950* featured some of the rarest toys ever pictured in any collectibles book, and *Cartoon Toys & Collectibles* marks his sixth work for Collector Books.

In addition to collectibles book writing, Longest is a regular monthly columnist for *Toy Trader* magazine with his "On the Toy Trail" column now reaching into its fourth year. He has also done feature writing for the *Tri-State Trader, Collectors Showcase* magazine, and *Antique Toy World* magazine to name only a few.

Longest is a teacher and drama director in his "real" other life, and he has just become a nationally published playwright with his new play, "Little Women of Orchard House," to be released this fall about the same time this collectibles book hits the store shelves. His wife, Ann, is also a theatre director and teacher, and his daughter, Claire, now 12, is a professional actress with many regional theatre credits.

The author often lectures on the history of antique toys and popular collectibles, has been a guest lecturer for antique seminars, and has appeared on local and regional network television shows promoting the collecting of antique Mickey Mouse, Donald Duck, Snow White, and Pinocchio toys. Any persons interested in contacting the author about items for sale should send a SASE with a clear photo of the item along with the asking price to David Longest, PO Box 2183, Clarksville, IN 47129

COLLECTOR RESOURCES

The following are reputable auction sources for cartoon, animation, and comic character toys. This author has dealt with these sources for more than a decade, and they are all honest, personable, and outstanding collector mail and phone bid auction sources.

HAKE'S AMERICANA AND COLLECTIBLES
PO Box 1444
York, PA 17405
(717)848-1333
Note: Hake's will send a free sample catalog filled with cartoon character merchandise to any new customer who mentions this book! Outstanding merchandise selection with attractive catalog. Ted Hake is a leader in the collectibles auction field.

SMITH HOUSE TOY SALES
PO Box 336
Eliot, Maine 03903
(207)439-4614
Note: Herb Smith puts out a full-color, gorgeous catalog often filled with cartoon character toys. An excellent resource for serious collectors!

NEW ENGLAND AUCTION GALLERY
PO Box 2273
W. Peabody, MA 01960-2273
Note: Debbie and Marty Crim produce a slick, colorful catalog that caters to serious toy collectors, including lots of great cartoon character toys.

CONTRIBUTING COLLECTOR PROFILES

Glenn Edwards is a talented former theatre director who has co-directed large scale theatrical productions with the author and now shares a collecting interest with his friend. Glenn is Looney over Warner Brothers characters, and in a five-year time span has amassed a wonderful toy collection of vintage Bugs Bunny, Elmer Fudd, and Daffy Duck items, to name only a few. Aside from being one of the author's very best friends, Glenn is also gaining quite a following as a toy and memorabilia dealer (among other things) on Ebay. Collectors who wish to contact him about Warner Brothers items he has for sale should go to his website on Ebay by entering his dealer code, gjcollect.

Ron Flick is an Indiana architect who also just happens to be a serious fan of Hanna-Barbera characters. His knowledge of all the vintage 1960s and 1970s Hanna-Barbera cartoons is a legacy that he has already passed on to his younger children, and his wonderful cartoon toys make up a big part of the Hanna-Barbera portion of this book. His little children were a joy to work with as they helped the author set up the photo shots for this book. Persons wishing to contact Ron about cartoon characters may do so by writing Ron Flick, c/o David Longest, PO Box 2183, Clarksville, IN 47129.

Dennis Frangipane is the owner of the South Louisville Antique and Toy Mall which graciously threw open its doors and showcases to the author to allow photography for this book. The Toy Mall features a wide variety of toys from the 1900s to the present and boasts literally hundreds of well-lit, new showcases filled to the brim with antique and collectible toys. The mall is one of the nation's fastest growing toy collector destinations, and toy collectors passing through Louisville, Kentucky, should contact Dennis at (502)955-5303. The Antique and Toy Mall is located at 4150-8 East Blue Lick Road, Louisville, KY 40229.

Doug Moore is one of central Indiana's most advanced cartoon and comic character collectors in addition to being a very knowledgeable antique advertising dealer and collector. Doug's taste leans toward the very rare and unique toys in outstanding condition. Some of the rare Disney and cartoon character Line Mar items pictured in this book came from Doug's outstanding collection. Aside from being an all-around great guy, Doug has been a good collecting friend of the author for over a decade. Persons wishing to contact him may do so by writing Doug Moore, 57 Hickory Ridge Circle, Cicero, IN 46034.

Inez Real is a devoted fan of Warner Brothers' Foghorn Leghorn (the really big rooster!) and all things relating to Teenage Mutant Ninja Turtles. Her collection started out to be a gathering of items for her grandchildren, but the collection in southern Indiana has grown to be one of truly "Mutant" proportions. It is her collection that makes up the heart of the Turtles pictured in this book, and the author thanks her for allowing him into her house on the evening of the Midwest's worst snowstorm in 100 years to do the photography of all those great little reptiles. Persons wishing to contact Inez regarding rare Ninja Turtle items, or any items for sale, may reach her at her e-mail address: eyereal@aol.com

Terry Stewart is an advanced collector with a real thing for rare and early Popeye and other comic character wind-ups. Stewart is a long-time collector of toys who has done his own share of helping the buyer meet the toys. As president of Stewart Promotions, Terry is at the helm of one of the nation's largest antique show and flea market promotion companies with shows in Indianapolis, Indiana, and Louisville, Kentucky, famous for indoor flea market extravaganzas with over 2,000 dealers. Terry is always interested in purchasing rare comic character items and serious sellers may contact him at (502)228-9646 (home) or (502)456-2244 (office).

Elmer and Viola Reynolds of central Indiana are advanced collectors of comic and cartoon collectibles who just happen to be author David Longest's dearest friends. Their toys have been featured in all of the author's six books, and their knowledge of the toy collecting field is impressive. As advanced collectors of character toys for nearly three decades, Elmer and Viola are always on the hunt for rare old Disneyana, Kewpie collectibles, cartoon and character memorabilia, and antique advertising. Persons wishing to contact them may do so care of the author, David Longest, PO Box 2183, Clarksville, IN 47129.

Mike Sullivan and Gena Lightle operate As Time Goes By, a trendy, upscale antique and pop culture store in Louisville's Historic Bardstown Road antique area. For nearly two decades they have specialized in antiques, dishes, pottery, and of course, vintage cartoon and character toys. Gena is a *Lady and the Tramp* collector who also likes Jiminy Cricket, among others. While their tastes range to the eclectic, the shop is an amazing place to visit because its wares change daily. Both contributed personal collection items (and store stock) to the pages of this book. Persons wishing to contact them may write Mike Sullivan, c/o As Time Goes By, 1310 Bardstown Road, Louisville, KY 40204 or phone him at (502)458-5774.

Schroeder's ANTIQUES Price Guide

. . . is the #1 best-selling antiques & collectibles value guide on the market today, and here's why . . .

• More than 450 advisors, well-known dealers, and top-notch collectors work together with our editors to bring you accurate information regarding pricing and identification.

• More than 45,000 items in almost 550 categories are listed along with hundreds of sharp original photos that illustrate not only the rare and unusual, but the common, popular collectibles as well.

• Each large close-up shot shows important details clearly. Every subject is represented with histories and background information, a feature not found in any of our competitors' publications.

• Our editors keep abreast of newly developing trends, often adding several new categories a year as the need arises.

8½ x 11, 612 Pages, $12.95

If it merits the interest of today's collector, you'll find it in *Schroeder's*. And you can feel confident that the information we publish is up to date and accurate. Our advisors thoroughly check each category to spot inconsistencies, listings that may not be entirely reflective of market dealings, and lines too vague to be of merit. Only the best of the lot remains for publication.

Without doubt, you'll find
SCHROEDER'S ANTIQUES PRICE GUIDE
the only one to buy for
reliable information and values.